SOCIOLOGY AND THE MILITARY ESTABLISHMENT

SAGE SERIES ON ARMED FORCES AND SOCIETY

INTER-UNIVERSITY SEMINAR ON ARMED FORCES AND SOCIETY

Morris Janowitz, *University of Chicago*
Chairman and Series Editor

Charles C. Moskos, Jr., *Northwestern University*
Associate Chairman and Series Editor

Sam C. Sarkesian, *Loyola University*
Executive Secretary

SOCIOLOGY AND THE

MILITARY ESTABLISHMENT

Third Edition

Morris Janowitz

in collaboration with
Roger W. Little

with an introduction to the Third Edition

 **SAGE PUBLICATIONS**   Beverly Hills / London

For information address:

SAGE PUBLICATIONS, INC.
275 South Beverly Drive
Beverly Hills, California 90212

SAGE PUBLICATIONS LTD
St George's House / 44 Hatton Garden
London EC1N 8ER

Printed in the United States of America

ISBN 0-8039-0214-X (cloth), 0-8039-0215-8 (paper)

Library of Congress Catalog Card No. 65-23742

FIRST PRINTING, THIRD EDITION

First Edition, April, 1959
Revised Edition, August, 1965
Reprinted, March, 1969
Third Edition, November, 1974

This volume is based upon a study originally prepared for the American Sociological Association.

CONTENTS

TABLES

INTRODUCTION TO THE THIRD EDITION

I FIRST PREPARED *Sociology and the Military Establishment* as an assessment of existing theoretical perspectives and as an inventory of research findings. The task in 1959 was manageable because the amount of relevant literature was limited. Subsequently, I collaborated with Roger Little, Professor of Sociology, University of Illinois, Circle Campus, and we issued a revised edition in 1965; and the task was still relatively feasible. However, in the fifteen-year period as a whole, there has been a marked increase in research on the sociology of military institutions, war, and peacekeeping. No doubt other fields in the social sciences have grown much more rapidly and have accumulated a more extensive data base. But the developments in sociology and in related disciplines have been extensive enough to transform the state of research on these subjects. An analytic assessment of the key concept of professionalization has been developed by Bengt Abrahamsson in *Military Professionalization and Political Power* (Beverly Hills: Sage Publications, 1972).

In fact, in order to present an overview of research trends, the Inter-University Seminar commissioned Roger Little to prepare a new inventory. He then edited the *Handbook of Military Institutions* (Beverly Hills: Sage Publications, 1971). This volume, over 600 pages long, deals with sixteen subject areas. A bibliographic review has been presented by Kurt Lang in *Military Institutions and the Sociology of War* (Beverly Hills: Sage Publications, 1972).

The growth of research and scholarly writing has been reflected in the publications of the Inter-University Seminar on

Armed Forces and Society, which have progressively taken on an interdisciplinary character. First, the Inter-University Seminar established an annual book program, in conjunction with Sage Publications, to disseminate research in progress: Volume I—Charles Moskos, *Public Opinion and the Military Establishment*, 1973; Volume II—Sam Sarkesian, *The Industrial-Military Complex: A Reassessment*, 1973; Volume III—Philippe C. Schmitter, *Military Rule in Latin America*, 1973; Volume IV—Catherine Kelleher, *Political-Military Systems*, 1974. Then, in 1974, the Inter-University Seminar announced the founding of a quarterly, *Armed Forces and Society: An Interdisciplinary Journal*, with an international board of editors and an advisory group.

These and other research activities have in effect "dated" the formulations presented originally in *Sociology and the Military Establishment*. But published monographs seem to have their own natural history. Republication appears justified, first, because it may serve as a document in the intellectual development of the subject. By reference to the contents of this monograph, scholars and research persons can judge the origin and reformulation of central issues and propositions. Second, *Sociology and the Military Establishment* represents a perspective on the sociology of military institutions under conscription in the context of Western advanced industrialism. The emerging literature, new directions, and new analyses require and reflect a focus on the military's adaptation to a markedly different system of manpower, authority, and organizational goals. The overview represented in this monograph can, I hope, serve as a baseline against which to assess the transformation of an institution.

In recent years, the focus of research on military institutions has responded to two fundamental historical trends. The first has been the shift from conscription toward a more extensive reliance on all-volunteer forces in Western parliamentary democracies—a shift which is not a temporary or short-term development. The other has been the emergence of the military forces as crucial ingredients in the political realities of the new nations of Africa, the Middle East, and Asia, and in the changing role of the military in Latin America as well.

The movement from conscription toward an all-volunteer force, especially in the United States, has long been anticipated by research scholars; it represents basic processes of technological and sociopolitical change. In one form or another, conscription is being modified, constricted, or abandoned by the Western industrialized nations with parliamentary political systems. This trend reflects: (a) the introduction of nuclear weapons; (b) the decline of Western colonial domination; and (c) the widespread resistance by segments of young people to the military style of life. The introduction of an all-volunteer manpower system implies a shift in military organization from a mobilization cadre for total war toward a force "in being" designed for deterrence.

An all-volunteer force raises persistent questions concerning the position of the military in a democratic society and its effective control by civilians. With the ending of the draft, the United States has had to face the question: who will serve as officers and enlisted personnel? A democratic society requires an armed force which is broadly representative of the larger society. But the all-volunteer force raises the possibility that the enlisted ranks, especially in the ground forces, will be filled by members of minority groups, with an overrepresentation of black and Spanish-speaking elements. In the officer corps, the potentials are for an increase in self-recruitment, with strong regional imbalances. As a result, the possible emergence of an officer corps with a selective civilian contact and distinct, if implicit, political orientation cannot be disregarded. An expanded all-volunteer military force—on a long-term basis—is a new development in American history which requires new research perspectives if effectiveness and civilian control are to be maintained.

The second development, the political role of the military in the developing nations, has produced extensive theorizing, and only slowly has the essential monographic literature on specific regimes been prepared. Samuel Huntington, in *Political Order in*

Changing Societies (New Haven: Yale University Press, 1968), has sought to characterize the accumulated literature as falling into one of two categories. In one group, there are supposed to be those writers who believe that military regimes come into power because of their specific internal organizational characters—especially their organizational discipline and resources. However, in Huntington's opinion, the more accurate view is that military regimes come into power because of breakdowns in civilian political systems. In effect, this arbitrary distinction bears little relation to the actual sociopolitical processes. The effective literature on this subject focuses on the sociopolitical developments which first bring about a deterioration of civilian regimes; and then the central issue is to explain why the military can assume power. At this point in the process, the internal characteristics of the military help account for its ability, in contrast to that of other groups, to seize power.

Furthermore, the explanation of the seizure of power by the military is less important than the issue of the performance —real and potential—of military regimes as "modernizers." Initially, a group of government policy planners, plus research personnel at government-supported research institutions, concluded that the military of the developing nations had important potentials for orderly modernization. However, alternative theoretical and empirical literature rapidly appeared which postulated the continued growth of military regimes with their instabilities and political defects. In particular, this alternative literature highlighted the limitations of such military regimes in creating the sociopolitical conditions necessary for economic growth. In this view, military regimes could be effective to the extent to which they took steps to develop civilian-based organizations which could exercise political influence and serve as a basis for developing political legitimacy.

Over the last fifteen years, research on military institutions —both on U.S. military institutions and those of other industrialized nations, as well as in the developing nations—has developed a more interdisciplinary character. Initially, it was psychologists who turned a research perspective on military institutions. As noted in this monograph, during World War I psychologists were involved in intelligence testing and personnel selection. While their tasks were apparently specific and operational, in effect these psychologists were dealing with central issues of profound importance and influence on their discipline. These research topics continue to command attention. During World War II, psychologists broadened their concern to include the analysis of morals and attitude formation, topics which again were of crucial importance to psychological analysis. Military psychology emerged from World War II as a fairly institutionalized specialty, but its analytic perspective remained relatively fixed until the first years of the 1970s. A new ferment has been operating which leads psychologists to be concerned with the psychology of organizational behavior as well as with professional and occupational socialization into the military.

After World War I, a new academic interest in the military rested with political scientists—a handful, at that—who were concerned with the study of war and with civil-military relations. These efforts were pioneered mainly by members of the Chicago realist school of politics—Quincy Wright and Harold D. Lasswell. Hans Speier, a German emigré sociologist, was one of the first in the United States to write on military institutions. The sociological interest which emerged as an aftermath of World War II reflected a concern with the analysis of bureaucratic organization and professions, as derived from the writings of Max Weber. The major interdisciplinary thrust since the first edition of *Sociology and the Military Establishment* has been the interpenetration of the sociological and political science perspectives. The extension of the sociopolitical perspective into the historical study of military affairs has been particularly important; tactical military history has become augmented by the analytic and comparative study of armed forces and society. There has also been an increase, although hardly an extensive one, in the legal study of military institutions.

In the interdisciplinary approach to the study of armed forces and society, economic analysis occupies an ambiguous position. The application of cost-benefit analysis to military operations has become a major effort. The procedures of statistical and economic analysis serve as management tools. They were developed during World War II and spread to industrial corporations. With the appointment of Robert McNamara as Secretary of Defense, these methods received a powerful impetus in the military setting. However, academic economists have not shown great interest in the economics of national defense except as an element in the pattern of federal expenditure.

While scholars struggle to develop analytic perspectives and to collect appropriate data, contemporary political and ideological considerations obviously influence their interests and outlook. The impact of nuclear weapons and the agonies of Vietnam have not only altered military doctrines, but have fashioned the language of social scientists. Research on military institutions fuses with the analysis of "conflict management." International relations as a discipline must confront new definitions concerning the acceptability and utility of military force. In this context, a group of researchers have arisen who call themselves "peace researchers." Examination of their scholarly, as opposed to their political and ideological perspectives, indicates a strong concern with attitude research and with social-psychological processes of communication in international relations. These aspects of peace research represent a continuity and refinement of central issues in the analysis of armed forces, peacekeeping, and conflict management.

Much has been made of the assertion that the study of military institutions has been strongly influenced by the financial resources available for such endeavors. However, it is necessary also to assert that the development of a topic of special interest only partially reflects budgetary support. In the social sciences, the intellectual attraction of a problem is important, and the sheer willingness of scholars to allocate time and effort in the context of their teaching responsibilities is an essential and almost overriding factor. The development of the sociology of military institutions in the United States has not been based on the extensive allocation of research funds, but on the core efforts of a group of cooperating scholars. Initially, governmental funding had little relation to the intellectual development except, perhaps, for supplying background documentation. Likewise, the enormous expansion of writing on the military in the new nations has not been based on extensive financial support. Of course, there comes a point at which the development of a research topic requires extensive research funds to test systematically crucial hypotheses.

By comparison with the financing for the physical and biological sciences, expenditures in the United States for the social sciences constitute a very small amount. This is not to imply that the social sciences are undersubsidized. Further, within the social sciences, expenditures for the study of military institutions consume a very small fraction as compared with the study of crime, mental health, and economic behavior. Moreover, the bulk of the funds for the study of the military institutions comes from the federal government, the Department of Defense and the military services. Most of the funds spent on the study of military institutions deal with internal organization, management, and personnel dimensions; only a very small portion focuses on the impact of U.S. military operations at home and abroad. The amount used in the comparative or cross-national study of military institutions is indeed tiny.

A science policy in the social sciences is difficult to develop and implement. In particular, there has been little effort to create a policy linking public and private funding that would enhance the social science staff of the military. As of 1974, the Social Science Research Council, the central clearinghouse for formulating social science objectives, has discontinued its efforts to deal with military institutions or civil-military relations. This is particularly noteworthy in the light of this group's strong involvement in the study of developing nations. In the area of comparative analysis, it is no doubt an advantage for the individual scholar to proceed on his own and in terms of mutual arrangements that he is able to develop with overseas colleagues. The support for research into military institutions from private foundations is very limited and appears, in fact, to have declined. The National Science Foundation completely avoids involvement and probably rightly so; in part it does not wish to "evaluate" the performance of U.S. military institutions.

The funds expended by the U.S. military to study itself are used to collect a vast array of statistical data, conduct numerous sample surveys, and sponsor social science research by its own personnel and, through contracts and grants, by universities, nonprofit research centers, and commercial groups. Military agencies, on a much more limited basis, support "policy studies" designed to assess alternative U.S. military strategies and plans. These studies are carried out by closely affiliated research institutes, generally on a "crash" basis. The bulk of their findings receive at best informal distribution; and, although they draw on social science and sociological concepts, their overall contribution to the social sciences is limited. They serve mainly as indicators of the focus of interest of official personnel in the Department of Defense.

The present state of the sociology of military institutions and conflict management in the United States reflects three decades of relations between academic researchers and the military establishment, relations which can hardly be characterized as effective or as guided by a set of responsible norms. Events such as "Project Camelot" and the prolonged agonies of Vietnam strained relations to the breaking point, but the difficulties had been operative since the end of World War II.

During World War II, total mobilization brought competent social scientists into a position in the military from which they could exercise a high degree of professional responsibility. They saw their commitment as limited to the duration of the conflict and were prepared for complete involvement during this period. The research data which were collected for presumed operational requirements supplied the basis for theoretically grounded scholarship finished after the end of the war. The national and ideological goals of World War II fused with the personal commitments of most of the social scientists.

After World War II, the military services developed social science units which believed that their objectives were to support "basic" social science as well as to do operational research. Although the distinction between basic and applied research cannot easily be applied to the social sciences, the military services did act for a number of years as a substitute for social science research funding by the National Science Foundation. But, appropriately, this responsibility was in time transferred from their jurisdiction.

One of the core issues involved in the military support of research hinged on the administration of funds. It was decided that the management and funding units for social science research would be placed under the military "research commands" which were directed by physical and biological scientists rather than being established as separate entities. This decision was in good measure supported and advocated by civilian social scientists, who believed that such an arrangement would result in stronger and more effectively budgeted programs. The decision generated grave strains, however, since the officials responsible for social science research did not have sufficient interest in and understanding of the limits and potentials of such research. Social science planning was forced to conform to models which were not necessarily appropriate. At various points, physical and biological science administrators also became "oversold" on the scope of the programs to be developed. The result was a high extent of instability and misunderstanding. Only slowly, over the years, have these programs developed a degree of stability. Basic issues in the appropriate management of social science remain an unsolved problem, although there has been a gradual trend to free it from control by "hard science" officials.

Progressively, after the end of World War II, tensions between academic social scientists and the military increased both because of administrative conflicts and, more profoundly, because of deepening political and ideological differences. The Korean conflict was a war of partial mobilization, and the military were unable to involve the most effective civilian talent. There was an unsuccessful effort to create a more permanent social science staff. The organizational structure of the military also imposed restraints on social science research to a much greater extent than during World War II. Nevertheless, some relevant data collection occurred that led to significant publications at a later date on the topics of race relations in the United States forces, on the battle morale of the communist forces, and on the behavior of U.S. prisoners of war. For example, the research by Albert Biderman, presented in *The Road of Calumny*, served as a powerful correction to the stereotypes in the mass media about how U.S. troops behaved in captivity.

In the period after the Korean War, the status of academic research on military institutions and the linkages between the university-based social scientists and the military establishment were to reach a critical threshold. The dominant trend, based on a failure to confront the basic professional and institutional issues, was to lead to violent tension between the military and the universities. On one level, this confrontation resulted from the widespread political opposition to the Vietnam War on university campuses that led to government-sponsored research being selected as an object of attack. Several prominent university professors who supported the war in Vietnam and were engaged in either consultation or research became special and pointed targets of protest.

However, on another and equally persistent level, the tension resulted from the failure to establish effective norms for relating university research personnel to government funding sources. This failure reflected administrative and professional defects in both parties. The government sponsored secret research on campuses while the universities erred in accepting such research, for secret research is incompatible with the goals of a civilian university. At times, the conditions under which funds were granted were unclear or involved such restrictions that the research could not be performed under the procedures of academic freedom, inquiry, and publication required by university norms. Again, the very fact that such research was being executed during a period of partial mobilization meant that many outstanding social scientists, those best equipped to deal with both the substantive and the procedural issues, did not become involved. Much of this research, if done at all, should have been done by government agencies rather than by university-based personnel.

Equally disruptive was the failure of university personnel to recognize the political context in which they were operating and to exercise their professional responsibilities. Effective research by university personnel must be separated from the actual or potential stigma of intelligence work. Those social scientists who became involved in Project Camelot were in error because they failed to insure that their efforts would meet this requirement, and therefore their preliminary work created undue political confusion and tension. They also erred deeply when they gave their approval to a research undertaking which had little intellectual feasibility—the idea that computer-based projects could predict revolutionary outbursts in Latin America was a grotesque distortion of the purposes and goals of social research.

As in the case of World War II and the Korean conflict, military officials during the Vietnam hostilities launched special social science data-collecting efforts to augment their regular operational reporting systems. These efforts were undoubtedly influenced and fashioned by the profound hostility of the university community to the war in Vietnam and by the refusal of the majority of social scientists to cooperate in research presumably designed to support operational requirements. One topic of central importance was the impact of air warfare, tactical and strategic, on civilian and military morale; and various research projects on this topic were conducted. The basic data which were collected have not been released, nor have any comprehensive analytical studies been published. Therefore, full assessment of these research efforts cannot be made. However, fragmentary materials which have been reported in the mass media indicate that they failed to confront the realities involved. Both research and military policy were launched without adequate reference to the findings of the Strategic Bombing Survey in Germany and Japan, or to the studies in Korea, that clearly concluded that air warfare has limited effects on morale.

The official, classified research findings in Vietnam initially exaggerated the impact of air warfare and, in fact, failed to highlight the reverse effect—namely, its positive contribution to the political control exercised by the Viet Cong and the North Vietnamese over their populations. Thus, the type of social science research which was developed in Vietnam ironically served to distort official perception of the realities of that conflict. Much, although not all, research sponsored by the military on Vietnam operations was difficult, if not impossible, to reconcile with the goals and procedures of a civilian university. It is notable that only an occasional scholar, such as Charles Moskos of Northwestern University, showed the appropriate initiative and professional responsibility and had himself accredited as a newspaper correspondent in order to pursue field research in Vietnam. As a result, social science research on military affairs, regardless of its sponsorship, came under widespread attack during the second half of the 1960s.

This dominant trend of tension and incomplete professional responsibility was predictably accompanied by a more circumscribed but persistent countertrend. The publication of *Sociology and the Military Establishment* in 1959 signaled the fact that there was a group of social scientists who, regardless of their policy outlook, wished to pursue research on military institutions on a scholarly basis and with professional responsibility. They believed that it was essential to continue intellectually objective analysis of military institutions and their impact on U.S. society and to make their findings available in scholarly publications. Through the years of confrontation and disruption of academic life, these social scientists were able to press forward with their research. On the basis of collegial support, they succeeded in maintaining and even expanding academic teaching and research on these vital issues. They relied mainly on their own labor power and some limited foundation support during the years of tension about government-sponsored research.

In time their conviction that the study of military institutions is an essential aspect of university intellectual life, and that it must be developed under conditions which insure professional and academic self-regulation, has become accepted. Professional arrangements have been established, such as the Inter-University Seminar on Armed Forces and Society, that have served to strengthen these efforts. This countertrend has emerged as the dominant approach. Thus the study of military institutions has been established as a university-based topic, distinct from government-conducted research. Its vitality cannot be dependent on government involvement in research, but must reflect academic interest and initiative. The core who persisted in their scholarly efforts during the 1960s gained recognition for their intellectual position, and the analysis of the military in the form of teaching and student research has moved more to the center of academic life on university campuses. This is hardly to assert that the conditions for self-generated university investigation of military institutions is satisfactory. It is, rather, to assert that, with the end of military operations in Vietnam and the introduction of the all-volunteer force, the context for research on these matters, including that supported by the government, has altered.

The end of conscription was a development which received widespread support among university faculties, but the problems of the all-volunteer force could not be avoided. Likewise, in the post-Vietnam period, the study of the military in the developing nations could be pursued without undue ideological agitation in the background. The most striking development is that university research centers which avoided or were opposed to military contracts and grants in the 1960s, such as the Institute for Social Research at the University of Michigan, have become actively involved in research on the social and psychological dimensions of the military manpower issues connected with the all-volunteer force.

The reduction in tensions between the military establishment and the university hardly implies a solution to the problems of federal support. Portions of the data collected by the military filter into the hands of academic scholars and supply essential documentation. Problems of race, drugs, and discipline during the final phases of the Vietnam conflict produced a sudden increase in funds for social research. The difficulties of implementing the all-volunteer force have resulted in increased expenditures by the military establishment for such research. However, there exists no adequate reporting system on the amount, scope, and subject matter for these efforts, and there is no adequate device for assessing their quality. Much of the funds is spent on collecting data for delimited and specific topics; the thrust is to measure the extent of a particular operational problem rather than to analyze its systemic character in depth. Very few of these studies find their way into academic or scholarly journals where they can be evaluated by existing research standards.

While the distinction between basic and applied research is an elusive one in the social sciences, it is clear that the pressure of day-to-day problems and the elaborate organization of research support lead the military to subsidize "operational" research which does not necessarily contribute either to a deeper understanding of military institutions or to the development of the social sciences. The analysis of findings and the development of explanatory modes are deemphasized. On balance, these data produce essential descriptive findings. But the long-term objectives of analytic investigation of military institutions appear to rest with "extra-military" scholars. No doubt any institution requires outside analysts. There is every reason to believe that, to a considerable measure, this task will remain with outside investigators, such as those affiliated with the Inter-University Seminar on Armed Forces and Society. However, the efforts of individual military officers at various service schools to turn their attention to such types of writing and analysis are striking.

In the 1960s, the temporary distortion of the academic endeavor resulted in pressure against independent scholars pursuing their own research into military institutions. In the post-Vietnam period, a different set of problems are emerging. Many military commanders are deeply concerned with research findings that may cause "bad" publicity and embarrass the efforts to develop the all-volunteer force; others believe that such research is necessary for formulating appropriate public policy in a free society. The result has been an increasing defensiveness on the part of some military authorities about releasing findings and permitting access to research. In particular, military officers engaged in relevant research have become more and more reluctant to press for clearance of their findings, some of which are crucial.

Likewise, it is understandable that research on the impact of the Vietnam War on the American military profession has been slow to emerge. The analysis of the effect of Vietnam impinges on the general study of social and political change in the United States and cannot be separated from it. At the heart of the analysis rests an organizational evaluation of the U.S. military operations in Vietnam and the strains which stalemate and demoralization produced. The military have not authorized or sponsored fundamental studies of this type. They did collect masses of data. Of particular importance are the materials on the pressures of smaller units during the final phases of military operations. In the years ahead, there is every reason to believe that persons involved in Vietnam may well produce detached analysis, and a new group of scholars may also become involved. But the basic analysis remains to be accomplished. For example, the patterns of demoralization need to be assessed: to what extent do existing theories apply to battle behavior in Vietnam? Adequate research on the social-class basis of conscription and of casualties has yet to be completed. Systematic research on the impact of Vietnam on military organization and on the cadres of the military profession, officers and noncommissioned officers, must be undertaken before it is too late. The one area in which research has been launched is the effect of their Vietnam experience on prisoners of war who have returned to the United States.

The amount of research sponsored by other federal agencies on military institutions and civil-military relations is very limited in comparison with the expenditures of the Department of Defense and the military services. The external research program of the Department of State periodically commissions research papers, while the U.S. Arms Control and Disarmament Agency sponsored, during the decade of the 1960s, a continuing program of university-based research; in the early 1970s, this program was markedly reduced. Its most important aspect was the worldwide data on military expenditures which have been collected by the staff of the agency itself and are published annually under the title, *World Military Expenditure.* The university-supported aspect of this program was mainly designed to assess policy alternatives. As the historian, Allan Millet, has concluded from a review of the research efforts of the U.S. Arms Control and Disarmament Agency, the scholarly residue has been limited (Allan Millet, "Armed Control Research and Military Institutions," *Armed Forces and Society: An Interdisciplinary Journal,* November 1974). The central weakness has been a failure to relate arms control to the structure and operation of military forces.

Military institutions are organized on the basis of nation-states and coalitions, voluntary and enforced, of nation-states. Scholarship has aspirations for international perspectives and international collaboration. The result is clearly inherent tensions in the study of military formations. Academic freedom is hardly a worldwide reality, and comparative perspectives easily become politicized. Any effort at collaborative research on military institutions and civil-military relations carries overtones of an intelligence operation, as well as the difficult problems of controlling personal and national bias. Given the barriers to the international study of military institutions, that which has been accomplished is most striking.

Such efforts reflect the initiative and thrust of individual scholars, but the work of the Research Committee on Armed Forces and Society of the International Sociological Association has supplied an important forum and vehicle for implementation. Comparative research has focused mainly on the developing nations, as scholars from the industrialized societies have sought to collaborate with their counterparts in the "new states." Few scholars from the latter areas have been able to cooperate and often only as political emigrés. The main thrust of such attempts has been to develop parallel case studies to be presented at international forums and in international publications.

International proceedings have been held in London (July 1964 and September 1967), Evian, France (September 1966), and Varna (September 1970). As a result, a series of special international publications has been prepared; "Armed Forces and Society in Western Europe" *European Journal of Sociology* (Archives européennes de sociologie), VI, No. 2 (1965); Jacques van Doorn, *Armed Forces and Society: Sociological Essays* (The Hague: Mouton, 1968); Jacques van Doorn, *Military Profession and Military Regimes* (The Hague: Mouton, 1968); Morris Janowitz and Jacques van Doorn, *On Military Intervention, On Military Ideology,* (Rotterdam: Rotterdam University Press, 1971). The emerging trend focuses more and more on comparisons among the industrialized nations.

It has always been the case that effective social science research must confront issues of goals and purpose. The development of nuclear weapons in the industrialized nations has raised fundamental issues of the legitimacy of military purpose and the acceptance of military intervention. In the NATO countries, the utility of military force is a topic of continuing debate, complicated by the difficult question of who will serve in the military. In the Warsaw Pact nations, military purpose is not publicly debated, although the issues cannot be completely muted. The very fact that the military forces of these nations have wide internal security objectives in their own countries and in those of their allies tends to perpetuate traditional definitions.

Because of the changed role of the military in international relations among industrialized nations in this period of nuclear weaponry, social scientists have started to question basic conceptions and categories of military strategy. In "Volunteer Armed Forces and Military Purposes" (*Foreign Affairs*, April 1972, pp. 427-443) and in "Toward a Redefinition of Military Strategy in International Relations" (*World Politics*, Summer 1974), I have sought to sketch the elements of the changed role of military forces in the search for detente and a reduction of the threat of both total and limited wars. The International Institute of Strategic Studies has conducted seminars aimed at probing these issues. The result is a first, halting effort to reconceptualize military strategy, not in terms of conventional destructive capacity, but in terms of the "stabilizing" versus the "destabilizing" impact of weapons on domestic and international relations.

Military force continues to be a crucial dimension of international relations, although it operates in narrow confines. The basic issue is whether it is possible to move beyond "deterrence," which is essentially a military conceptualization, toward a more comprehensive analysis of the military's sociopolitical role. If deterrence must rest on the doomsday momentum of an unrestricted nuclear arms race, the results can only be undue international tension and profound international destabilization. There is no reason why military strategists cannot and should not build hypothetical models of a "world without war"—for such models can contribute to the next steps in arms control, international peacekeeping, and a realistic understanding of the positive and negative roles of force in international relations. In the continuing search for such an outlook, the categories of strategy and social science become fused. But social science concepts cannot be based on mechanical, cybernetic, or electronic analogues, but on concepts of institution building and purposeful leadership.

In preparing this third publication of *Sociology and the Military Establishment*, I have had the assistance of my colleagues in updating the bibliography.

Morris Janowitz

Chapter 1

THE MILITARY ESTABLISHMENT
AS A SOCIAL SYSTEM

IT IS APPROPRIATE to inquire why sociological literature on military organization has been slow to develop as compared, for example, with that on industrial and factory organization. To mention another example, the sociological research literature on the mental hospital is much more intensive than that available on military organization. This striking imbalance is particularly noteworthy because of the intense interest and critical debate on existing sociological findings about military institutions by both professional officers and civilian experts.

A good deal of effort has been expended by social scientists—mainly personnel and social psychologists—on very selected and specific aspects of military life. During World War I a relatively new approach to the use of military personnel was stimulated by social research, namely, the importance of considering a person's intelligence, skills, and aptitudes in assigning him to a military occupation. The experiences of military psychologists of this period provided a basis for the subsequent rapid development of personnel selection in civilian industry and business.

For better or for worse, during World War II an elaborate machinery was erected for matching men's skills to the jobs required. No large-scale organization as vast as the military establishment can operate without a standardized personnel selection system. But any personnel testing procedure runs the risk of developing over-specialization in both training procedures and personnel. It has even been argued that military personnel selection, as administered during World War II, resulted in draining off superior talent from essential but "unglamorous"

25

assignments, such as the infantry. Moreover, no responsible personnel selector will claim that the dimensions of aggressive leadership in combat or strategic command have been satisfactorily
conceptualized to the point where reliable personnel testing is
possible.

Thus it was understandable that during World War II social
scientists broadened their interests beyond personnel selection
and stressed the importance of research into motives and attitudes
as aspects of military life. Research on "morale" was by no means
a new approach to the management of complex and large-scale
organizations. But the armed forces, that is, the ground and air
forces, undertook morale studies on a most extensive scale. In the
summary study of these efforts, *The American Soldier*,[1] prepared
under the guidance of Samuel A. Stouffer, the potentialities and
limitations of attitude and morale research are assessed. And
again, as with the development of personnel selection during
World War I, industry and business have continued the morale
study as a tool of administrative management.

"MORALE" VERSUS ORGANIZATION

Social research on attitudes and morale in the armed forces
provides useful information for specific problems where it is
assumed that the execution of a policy requires cooperation. The
limitation of attitude research is not that the strategy and tactics
of war cannot be based on the preferences of soldiers. This is
obvious to all, including the social scientist. But, in fact, attitude
research fails to describe the underlying social system—the
realities of bureaucratic organization—of the armed forces.
"Morale" is much too limited a concept to understand the
coercive forces of bureaucratic organization, especially of military
formations as they operate in combat. The findings of *The
American Soldier* studies serve to underline and reaffirm this
sociological observation:

> Thus we are forced to the conclusion that personal motives and
> relationships are not uniquely determinate for organization in com-
> bat . . . officers and men must be motivated to make the organiza-
> tion work, but not *all* of them have to be so motivated, nor must they

all agree on details of social philosophy or be bound by ties of personal friendship in order for a functioning organization to exist. To put it another way, the best single predictor of combat behavior is the simple fact of institutionalized role: knowing that a man is a soldier rather than a civilian. The soldier role is a vehicle for getting a man into the position in which he has to fight or take the institutionally sanctioned consequences.[2]

A potential model for analyzing the military establishment as a social system is represented by social research into industrial organization, which has a broader tradition than personnel selection and morale studies. Intellectual influences from historical writings, economic analysis, social anthropology, and sociological theory have emphasized the need for a comprehensive focus on the totality of industrial organization, not merely on part of it. The single concept of "morale" is displaced by a theory of organizational behavior in which an array of sociological concepts is employed: authority, communications, hierarchy, sanction, status, social role, allocation, and integration. Industrial organizations have common patterns of behavior which can be traced to similarities in their technological apparatus and to their goals of profits and productivity. Alternatively, variations in industrial behavior can be linked to the cultural, ideological, and political facets of any particular society. The sociological perspective toward the industrial establishment has produced a wide variety of rich theoretical treatises and empirical case studies on the internal administration of the factory system, and on the impact of industrial organization on contemporary social structure.[3]

By contrast, there exist few comprehensive sociological statements on contemporary American military organization, although fragmentary theoretical essays and particularistic research studies abound.[4] One might assume that sociologists' aspirations for an understanding of modern social structures would force them into a concern with military institutions which so thoroughly pervade contemporary society. In recent years a sustained interest in military institutions has increased, and the subject is even being acknowledged in the standard introductory sociological texts. The origin of academic interest in this subject can be seen in the writings of such leading political sociologists as Harold D. Lasswell and Hans Speier, who have manifested a continuing and systematic concern with the implications of military organization as agents of social change.[5] One of the most insightful and penetrating analyses of American military behavior is contained in *Men Against Fire* by Brigadier General S. L. A. Marshall (Ret.).[6] Since he is a professional newspaper writer and a military historian, his writings are not explicitly sociological, but they are based on an intimate understanding of military social organization. Through data from group interviews with World War II soldiers immediately after combat and on direct observation of battle performance, Marshall sought to account for the low expenditure of firepower by combat units (less than one-quarter of the troops fired their weapons in battle).

Interestingly, the operational requirements of political warfare against the German and Japanese armed forces led to research efforts in which these forces were regarded as total social systems. During World War II two social science units, working independently, recast operational and strategic intelligence into sociological models for explaining the strength and vulnerability of the Axis armed forces as they came under allied attack.[7] Their findings, as well as those reported in *The American Soldier*, showed high convergence in underscoring the central importance of primary group solidarity even in totalitarian armies as a crucial source of military effectiveness. Specifically, a social system perspective helped to focus attention on the important conclusion that it was not Nazi ideology which was at the root of German fanatical resistance, but rather the military and organizational practices which the Nazis permitted, encouraged, and required.

Since the end of World War II, support of social science research, including sociological work, by the military establishment has grown tremendously in a pattern following the proliferation of such efforts in civilian institutions. To the outside observer, it would appear that this development has been at times sporadic and without effective forethought. To be sure, the growth of social science in the military has been beset by organizational rivalries, difficulties, and confusion. Such research has had to confront shortages of trained and committed personnel. At times, military agencies have undertaken projects in competition with civilian agencies so that important military topics were neglected. But a definite pattern of growth has emerged. The result is a body of findings about military institutions—fragmentary though they may be—without which it would be impossible to assemble this volume and speak of a sociological analysis of the military establishment.

The diffuse structure which has emerged for social science and sociological research in the armed forces articulates with the structure of the military establishment. At the level of the Department of Defense, there has been since 1947 a series of civilian-dominated groups charged with planning and coordinating social science research. The impact of these groups has been limited to fostering support for increased funds and identifying important and priority objectives. In each of the three major services, there is a centralized research office which grants funds, including funds for social science research, to civilian groups. In order to establish their position among civilian scientists, these agencies have striven to operate as general research-granting agencies, and much of their work in the past has complemented civilian agencies of the government and even private foundation grants. These agencies have also operated to support strategic studies for which the Department of State could not mobilize funds. In recent years these central research offices of the military services have become increasingly interested in fundamental research on the military environment and on military organization.

Relevant research on military institutions and military operations by social scientists is done by quasi-independent agencies established by the military services, such as The Rand Corporation (Department of the Air Force) or Special Operations Research Office (Department of the Army), and by "in-service" laboratories and study groups as well as by operating military units. At times, the formal arrangements are of little consequence, since some of the most important work has been done under extreme pressure by composite groups on various detached arrangements.

There is, of course, a division of labor that emerges between these various research agencies. The semi-independent research agencies, with extensive civilian contacts, concentrate on politico-military topics such as psychological warfare, the study of foreign areas, the military in the emerging nations, and unconventional types of warfare. The "in-service" and specialized laboratories deal with specific operational problems such as selection and survival training as well as manpower and personnel systems. Military staff agencies make use of social science techniques to collect basic information. Thus all of the services conduct on a periodic and continuing basis sample surveys of active duty personnel which parallel the wartime studies of attitude, information, and manpower characteristics.

The requirements of congressional and executive control of the armed forces have also resulted in special study groups which have generated important sociological data. A University of Michigan group investigated military retirement pay and assembled basic analyses on career commitment in the armed forces.[8] In 1964 a comprehensive study involving both military and university experts was launched in connection with the selective service matters. In recent years university-based research on military institutions has centered, in part, in the work of the Inter-University Seminar on Armed Forces and Society at the University of Chicago, sponsored by Russell Sage Foundation and the Social Science Research Council. The research compendium, *The New Military: Changing Patterns of Organization*, prepared by this group, presents the work of various sociologists concerned with the impact of technology on the military profession.[9]

In explaining the slow growth of a sustained and realistic interest in military institutions, professional sociologists are prone to argue that the military has resisted organizational studies, and particularly organizational studies that have sought to reach into the upper levels of military management. This is a partially correct observation, which is basically irrelevant. The assent of the military would facilitate sociological inquiry, but such assent is hardly indispensable. Some of the best analyses of industrial sociology have come from documentary and secondary sources, participant observation, and the careful use of informants— reluctant or otherwise.

In part, this defense by sociologists is incorrect. The military establishment has invited and subsidized social scientists to investigate fundamental problems of military organization. It is true that all too often this support has been sporadic and based on an exaggerated notion of the potentialities of social science. Some of these efforts have produced relevant results. However, many major endeavors have resulted in unfinished research, mimeographed reports of pilot projects, or trivial research contributions, which indicate that failures in contract research have, in part, been due to the social scientist.

The explanation for the present state of sociological analysis of the military establishment is more fundamental. In the United States the development of the social sciences is linked to the liberal tradition which, in general, has sought to handle the problem of military institutions by denial. There has been an understandable but fundamental tension between the professional soldier and the scholar, who seeks to apply the scientific method to the human side of military organization and armed conflict. The professional soldier often sees the social scientist as naive, even though he must defer to him because of professional courtesy. The social scientist sees the professional soldier as dogmatic. As a result, the approach of the social scientist to the military establishment has been segmental and technical, rather than comprehensive and scientific.

This issue can be stated in other terms. Civilian sociologists think of their relations with military officers in administrative terms without sufficient concern for the intellectual issues at stake. A university professor who prepares a research study or serves as a consultant evaluates the impact of his efforts in terms of its immediate consequences. First he asks the question: "What 'action' was taken?" More basic questions are often unasked. It is also necessary to judge the research in terms of its contribution to sociological knowledge. And even more important, the question must be asked: "What are its long-term consequences on military thinking? What basic questions and intellectual discussion, if any, did it raise?'

There is a long tradition of study of research reports by military staff planners and at the higher schools of the military establishment. The findings of social science have become part of this process. Such discussion takes place within the frame of reference of the military profession, but it is in part a reflective response to social science research, which in the long run helps to fashion and refashion the profession.

In fact, the military profession is very deeply involved in this process of self-scrutiny because of the complexity and gravity of the problems it faces. One might argue that there is as much self-scrutiny in the military profession as in many other professions and certainly more than in some; for example, the medical profession. There is an almost exaggerated hope and expectation in the published writings of civilian scholars and a rush to keep abreast of the most recent thinking. One specific result has been that the military more than other professions has incorporated an explicit analysis of its professional structure, including the elements of an sociological analysis, into its training and indoctrination. Thus *The Professional Soldier: A Social and Political Portrait*[10] has rapidly become an integral part of the intellectual life of the military establishment, and it is analyzed and criticized by each new generation of officers at various levels in the hierarchy.

In the past, an additional barrier to the development of sociological research on the military has been the view with which many social scientists have approached the armed forces; namely, they have held an orientation which was partly an expression of civilian ideology. As Hans Speier points out in his critique of the *The American Soldier* research series, such a view distorts actual differences between military and civilian organization, since it overlooks what is common to large-scale organization in general.[11] Many of the "bureaucratic" features of military life are, in fact, to be found in civilian organizations in varying degree. However, in the past, sociological analysis of military organization did not take into account the vast transformations that have occurred in the military and therefore continued to emphasize authoritarian, stratified-hierarchical, and traditional dimensions as a basis for distinguishing the military from the nonmilitary bureaucracy.[12]

For example, Campbell and McCormack in their study, "Military Experience and Attitudes Toward Authority,"[13] set out with the assistance of a United States Air Force research contract to prove that air cadet training would increase authoritarian predispositions among the officer candidates. Since they assumed that the dominant characteristics of a military organization are its authoritarian procedures, the consequences of participation in its training program necessarily heighten authoritarian personality tendencies among those who successfully pass through such training. Appropriately, authoritarian personality tendencies imply both the predisposition to dominate arbitrarily others of lower status and simultaneously to submit to arbitrary higher authority. When the results of the research, as measured by the well-known authoritarian "F" scale, showed a decrease in authoritarian traits among cadets after one year of training, the authors were tempted to conclude that perhaps their research tools were inadequate.[14] Direct examination of the organizational processes of combat flight training would indicate an emphasis on group interdependence and on a team concept of coordination to ensure survival that should have cautioned these researchers not to make the predictions they did make.[15] However, in the past decade, civilian scientists have markedly increased their capacity to formulate research designs applicable to military institutions.

BUREAUCRACY: CIVILIAN OR MILITARY

To analyze the contemporary military establishment as a social system, it is therefore necessary to assume that for some time it has tended to display more and more of the characteristics typical of any large-scale nonmilitary bureaucracy. The decreasing difference is a result of continuous technological change which vastly expands the size of the military establishment, increases its interdependence with civilian society, and alters its internal social structure. These technological developments in war-making require more and more professionalization. At the same time, the impact of military technology during the past half-century can be described in a series of propositions about social change. Each of the conditions symbolized by these propositions has had the effect of "civilizing" military institutions and of blurring the distinction between the civilian and the military. Each of these trends has, of course, actual and potential built-in limitations.

1. An increasing percentage of the national income of a modern nation is spent for the preparation, execution, and repair of the consequences of war. Thus there is a secular trend toward total popular involvement in the consequences of war and war policy, since the military establishment is responsible for the distribution of a progressively larger share of the available economic values. However, there is some evidence that with the development of "atomic plenty," direct military budgets of the major powers tend to level off. Indirect costs continue to grow, but it is difficult to estimate whether military expenditures as a proportion of the gross national product will continue to increase.

2. Military technology both vastly increases the destructiveness of warfare and widens the scope of automation in new weapons. It is a commonplace that both of these trends tend to weaken the distinction between military roles and civilian roles as the destructiveness of war has increased. Weapons of mass destruction socialize danger to the point of equalizing the risks of warfare for both soldier and civilian. As long as the armed forces must rely on drafted personnel, powerful influences toward civilianization are at work. However, there are limits to this trend, particularly in that actual limited war operations are already carried out only by professional personnel. While it seems problematic to achieve, the notion of a fully professional armed force in the United States without selective service became in 1965 a topic for political debate.

3. The revolution in military technology means that the military mission of deterring violence becomes more and more central as compared with preparing to apply violence. This shift in mission tends to civilianize military thought and organization as military leaders concern themselves with broad ranges of political, social, and economic policies.

4. The previous periodic character of the military establishment (rapid expansion, rapid dismantlement) has given way to a more gradual and continuous pattern of adjustment. The permanent character of the military establishment has removed one important source of civilian-military conflict, namely, the civilian tendency to abandon the military establishment after a war. Instead, because of the high rate of technological change, internal conflicts between the military services have been multiplied.

5. The complexity of the machinery of warfare and the requirements for research, development, and technical maintenance tend to weaken the organizational boundary between the military and the nonmilitary, since the maintenance and manning of new weapons require a greater reliance on civilian-oriented technicians. The counter-trend, or at least limitation, is the greater effort by the military establishment to develop and train military officers with scientific and engineering backgrounds.

6. Given the "permanent" threat of war, it is well recognized that the tasks which military leaders perform tend to widen. Their technological knowledge, their direct and indirect power, and their heightened prestige result in their entrance, of necessity, into arenas that in the recent past have been reserved for civilian and professional politicians. The need that political and civilian leaders have for expert advice from professional soldiers about the strategic implications of technological change serves to mix the roles of the military and the civilian. But civilian leadership has in the past decade demonstrated great vigor and ability to give strategic direction and management to the armed forces. It would be accurate to state that while the roles of the professional military have broadened, civilian control and direction have been able to adapt to these changed circumstances.

Thus these observations do not deny the crucial differences that exist between military and nonmilitary bureaucracies. The goals of an organization supply a meaningful basis for understanding differences in organizational behavior. The military establishment as a social system has unique characteristics because the possibility of hostilities is a permanent reality to its leadership. The fact that thermonuclear weapons alter the role of

see P. 40

force in international relations does not deny this proposition. The consequences of preparation for future combat and the results of previous combat pervade the entire organization. The unique character of the military establishment derives from the requirement that its members are specialists in making use of violence and mass destruction. In the language of the soldier, this is recognized on a common-sense basis: military mission is the key to military organization.

Changing technology creates new patterns of combat, and thereby modifies organizational behavior and authority in the military establishment. The narrowing distinction between military and nonmilitary bureaucracies can never result in the elimination of fundamental organizational differences. Three pervasive requirements for combat set limits to these civilianizing tendencies.

First, while it is true that modern warfare exposes the civilian and the soldier to more equal risks, the distinction between military roles and civilian roles has not been eliminated. Traditional combat-ready military formations need to be maintained for limited warfare. The necessity for naval and air units to carry on the hazardous tasks of continuous and long-range reconnaissance and detection, demand organizational forms that will bear the stamp of conventional formations. In the future, even with fully automated missile systems, conventional units must be maintained as auxiliary forces for the delivery of new types of weapons.

More important, no military system can rely on expectation of victory based on the initial exchange of firepower, whatever the form of the initial exchange may be. Subsequent exchanges will involve military personnel—again regardless of their armament— who are prepared to carry on the struggle as soldiers, that is, subject themselves to military authority and to continue to fight. The automation of war civilized wide sectors of the military establishment; yet the need to maintain combat readiness and to develop centers of resistance after initial hostilities ensures the continued importance of military organization and authority.

Second, what about the consequences of the increased importance of deterrence as a military mission? Should one not expect that such a shift also would result in civilianizing the military establishment? If the military is forced to think about deterring wars rather than fighting wars, the traditions of the "military mind," based on the inevitability of hostilities, must change and military authority must undergo transformation as well. There can be no doubt that this shift in mission is having important effects on military thought and organization. In fact, military pragmatism which questions the inevitability of total war is an important trend in modern society as the destructiveness of war forces military leaders to concern themselves with the political consequences of violence.

Again, there are limits to the consequences of this civilianizing trend. The role of deterrence is not a uniquely new mission for the military establishment. Historically, the contribution of the military to the balance of power has not been made because of the civilian character of the military establishment. To the contrary, the balance of power formula operates, when it does, because the military establishment is prepared to fight effectively and immediately.

With the increase in the importance of deterrence, military elites become more and more involved in diplomatic and political warfare, regardless of their preparation for such tasks. Yet the specific and unique contribution of the military to deterrence is the threat of violence which has currency; that is, it can be taken seriously because of the real possibility of violence. Old or new types of weapons do not alter this basic formula. In short, deterrence still requires organization prepared for combat.

Third, the assumption that military institutions, as compared with economic and industrial institutions, are resistant to technological change is considerably undermined as the process of innovation in the military establishment itself has become routinized. Nevertheless, as long as imponderables weigh heavy in estimating military outcomes and as long as the "fighter" spirit is required to face combat, the military rejects the civilian engineer as its professional model. Of course, the engineer is held in high esteem, but the ideal image of the military continues to be the strategic commander, not the military technician. It is the image of a leader, motivated by national patriotism and not by personal monetary gain, who is capable of organizing the talents of specialists for all types of contingencies.

Likewise, leadership based on traditional military customs must share power with experts not only in technical matters but also in matters of organization and human relations. Specific organizational adaptations of the military even foreshadow developments in civilian society, since the military must press hard for innovation and respond more rapidly to social change. For example, the continued need for retraining personnel from operational to managerial positions and from older to newer techniques has led to a more rational spreading of higher education throughout the career of the military officer, rather than the concentrated dosage typical of the civilian in graduate or professional school.

No bureaucracy ever conforms to the ideal model of the rational organization and certainly the military establishment cannot be thought of in purely engineering terms. As long as "the battle is the pay off"—as long as there are dangerous and irksome tasks to be performed—an engineering philosophy cannot suffice as the organizational basis of the armed forces. Especially in a free enterprise, profit-motivated society, the military establishment is oriented to duty and honor. S. L. A. Marshall's observations express this essential theme of military life:

> A note of smugness was not missing from the remark all too frequently heard during World War II: "We go at this thing just like it was a great engineering job." What was usually overlooked was that to the men who were present at the pay off, it wasn't an engineering job, and had they gone about their duty in that spirit, there would have been no victory for our side.[16]

These trends in self-concepts and roles are described and analyzed in *The Professional Soldier: A Social and Political Portrait*, as they have affected the officer corps during the past half-century in the United States.[17] The military profession which has centered on the self-conception of the warrior type, or the "heroic leader" requires the incorporation of new roles, namely, the "military manager" and the "military technologist." For the military establishment to accomplish its multiple goals, it must develop and maintain a balance between these different military types.

These basic changes in the military over the past fifty years can be summarized by a series of basic propositions on the transformation of military organization in response both to the changing technology of war and to the transformation of the societal context in which the armed forces operate.[18]

1. *Changing Organizational Authority.* There has been a change in the basis of authority and discipline in the military establishment, a shift from authoritarian domination to greater reliance on manipulation, persuasion, and group consensus. The organizational revolution which pervades contemporary society, and which implies management by means of persuasion, explanation, and expertise, is also to be found in the military.

2. *Narrowing Skill Differential Between Military and Civilian Elites.* The new tasks of the military require that the professional officer develop more and more of the skills and orientations common to civilian administrators and civilian leaders. The narrowing difference in skill between military and civilian society is an outgrowth of the increasing concentration of technical specialists in the military.

3. *Shift in Officer Recruitment.* The military elite has been undergoing a basic social transformation since the turn of the century. These elites have been shifting their recruitment from a narrow, relatively high social status base to a broader base, more representative of the population as a whole.

4. *Significance of Career Patterns.* Prescribed careers performed with high competence lead to entrance into the professional elite, the highest point in the military hierarchy at which technical and routinized functions are performed. By contrast, entrance into the smaller group, the elite nucleus—where innovating perspectives, discretionary responsibility, and political skills are required—is assigned to persons with unconventional and adaptive careers.

5. *Trends in Political Indoctrination.* The growth of the military establishment into a vast managerial enterprise with increased

political responsibilities has produced a strain on traditional military self-images and concepts of honor. The officer is less and less prepared to think of himself as merely a military technician. As a result, the profession, especially within its strategic leadership, has developed a more explicit political ethos.

In a period of fantastic technological change, military leadership is confronted with an almost perpetual crisis of organization. The sociological analyst is concerned with understanding the organizational consequences of these technological changes. Yet it can be assumed that neither the increased automation of military technology, nor the military shift in mission from war-making to deterrence, nor the decline in the traditional military opposition to innovation can produce a complete civilianization of the military establishment. The structure of military authority —the key to military organization—is an expression of the unique goals of the military, namely, combat and combat preparation.

In terms of mass destruction, air power is the ascendant arm, while ground and sea power remain the essential components of a system of graduated deterrence. The diversification and specialization of military technology lengthens the formal training required to gain mastery of military technology. The temporary citizen soldier, sailor, and aviator will become less important and a completely professional armed force more vital. The need to fight limited wars or deter strategic wars instantly, with the available mobilized forces, tends to increase reliance on a professional military establishment. Likewise, the military becomes involved in a variety of functions, such as counter-insurgency, military assistance programs, para-military activities, and even nation-building by means of civic action. But these contemporary trends do not produce a professional armed force isolated and remote from civilian society. Rather, it is a military establishment that is an integral part of the larger society on which its technological resources depend.

NOTES TO CHAPTER 1

1. Stouffer, Samuel A., and others, *The American Soldier*. Princeton University Press, Princeton, N.J., 1949, vols. 1 and 2.

2. *Ibid.*, vol. 2, p. 101.

3. The main impetus for these analyses of the industrial establishment has not been the immediate solution of any practical problem. Rather, it is that an understanding of contemporary society is impossible without such an interest.

4. Efforts in this direction are contained in Andrzejewski, Stanislaw, *Military Organization and Society*, Routledge and Kegan Paul, London, 1954; Williams, Richard Hays, *Human Factors in Military Operations: Some Applications of the Social Sciences to Operations Research*, Technical Memorandum ORO-T-259, Operations Research Office, Chevy Chase, Md., 1954, mimeographed; *Report of the Working Group on Human Behavior Under Conditions of Military Service:* A Joint Project of the Research and Development Board and the Personnel Policy Board in the Office of the Secretary of Defense, Washington, June, 1951; van Doorn, Jac A. A., *Sociologie van de organisatie: beschouwingen over organiseren in het bijzonder gebaseerd op een onderzoek van het militaire system*, H. E. Stenfert Kroese, Leiden, 1956.

5. Lasswell, Harold, *Politics: Who Gets What, When, How*, The Free Press, Glencoe, Ill., 1951; Speier, Hans, *Social Order and the Risks of War*, George W. Stewart, New York, 1952.

6. Marshall, S. L. A., *Men Against Fire*. William Morrow and Co., New York, 1947.

7. Leighton, Alexander, *Human Relations in a Changing World*, E. P. Dutton and Co., New York, 1949; Shils, Edward A., and Morris Janowitz, "Cohesion and Disintegration in the Wehrmacht in World War II," *Public Opinion Quarterly*, vol. 12, Summer, 1948, pp. 280–315.

8. U.S. Congress, Senate Committee on Armed Services, *A Study of the Military Retired Pay System and Certain Related Subjects*. 87th Congress, 1st Sess., Government Printing Office, Washington, 1961.

9. Janowitz, Morris, editor, *The New Military: Changing Patterns of Organization*. Russell Sage Foundation, New York, 1964.

10. Janowitz, Morris, *The Professional Soldier: A Social and Political Portrait*. The Free Press, Glencoe, Ill., 1960.

11. Speier, Hans, "The American Soldier and the Sociology of Military Organization" in Merton, Robert K., and Paul F. Lazarsfeld, editors, *Studies in the Scope and Method of "The American Soldier."* The Free Press, Glencoe, Ill., 1950, pp. 106–132.

12. Stouffer, Samuel A., and others, *op. cit.*, vol. 1, p. 55; Davis, Arthur K., "Bureaucratic Patterns in the Navy Officer Corps," *Social Forces*, vol. 27, December, 1948, pp. 143–153; Rose, Arnold M., "The Social Structure of the Army," *American Journal of Sociology*, vol. 51, March, 1946, pp. 361–364; Freeman, Felton D., "The Army as a Social Structure," *Social Forces*,

vol. 27, October, 1948, pp. 78–83; Brotz, Howard, and Everett Wilson, "Characteristics of Military Society," *American Journal of Sociology*, vol. 51, March, 1946, pp. 371–375; Spindler, G. Dearborn, "The Military: A Systematic Analysis," *Social Forces*, vol. 27, October, 1948, pp. 83–88; Page, Charles H., "Bureaucracy's Other Face," *Social Forces*, vol. 25, October, 1946, pp. 88–94.

13. Campbell, Donald T., and Thelma H. McCormack, "Military Experiences and Attitudes Toward Authority," *American Journal of Sociology*, vol. 62, March, 1957, pp. 482–490. The data were collected for this study during the period January, 1953, to March, 1954.

14. Adorno, T. W., and others, *The Authoritarian Personality*. Harper and Bros., New York, 1950, pp. 222–280.

15. In fact, there is some empirical evidence, as well as ample observations, that selection boards in the Air Force tend to select for promotion the less authoritarian officers, presumably in part through selecting well-liked men. See E. P. Hollander's "Authoritarianism and Leadership Choice in a Military Setting," *Journal of Abnormal and Social Psychology*, vol. 49, July, 1954, pp. 365–370. Richard Christie found only a slight and statistically insignificant increase in authoritarianism (California F scale) among a group of Army inductees after six weeks of infantry basic training; see *American Psychologist*, "Changes in Authoritarianism as Related to Situational Factors," vol. 7, June, 1952, pp. 307–308.

16. Marshall, S. L. A., *op. cit.*, p. 210.

17. Janowitz, Morris, *The Professional Soldier*, pp. 7–16.

18. *Ibid.*, pp. 21–36.

Chapter 2

HIERARCHY AND AUTHORITY

HIERARCHY is the hallmark of a sociological conception of bureaucratic organization. The principle of hierarchy is simply that every lower office is under the control and supervision of a higher one. Since by definition the military establishment is a comprehensive and an all-embracing hierarchy, the career soldier is assumed to be an ideal example of the professional operating under bureaucratic authority. The contemporary growth of bureaucratic organization in government, industry, and education implies the growth of this same hierarchical principle, historically associated with military life.

For the professional officer who has a career commitment to the military, or for the selective service recruit scheduled to spend a two-year tour of duty, military hierarchy operates pervasively. The professional officer has entered on a career that attaches him to a single authority through which all of his life chances are regulated. The recruit finds that the full cycle of his daily existence is now for the first time under the control of a single authority. Military life is, in short, institutional life.

However, the sources from which military authority derives power and influence are of crucial consequence. Does authority flow from custom, law, or the personal characteristics of a key officer, following the analytic categories of Max Weber? Do the systems of authority operate to reinforce each other, or do they operate to create organizational strains? How appropriate is the actual hierarchy of authority for the tasks and goals of the organization? No hierarchical organization of any size or complexity has an authority system based on a single principle. Hence the sociologist is concerned with the types of authority that predominate in the military establishment and the linkages between the various hierarchies of authority. In the past, authority in the military profession has been rooted in custom, tradition, law, and heroic achievement. To understand the changing patterns of authority in the military establishment, the sociologist directs attention to changes in the skill and rank structure, the status system, and the techniques of discipline. Each of these dimensions introduces new strengths and new strains in authority patterns in the military.

THE SKILL STRUCTURE

One approach to understanding the sources of organizational authority is to analyze the division of labor—the skill structure—in the military establishment. It is revealing to contrast the complex skill structure of a modern professional military organization—either under democratic or totalitarian political control—with the simple division of labor of the feudal armed force.[1] We can speak of the feudal or aristocratic type of military establishment as a composite model of western European military organization before industrialism began to have its full impact. Survivals of these forms have persisted in most military establishments during the twentieth century.

The most striking aspect of the skill structure of the aristocratic military establishment was its close articulation with the then existing larger society. The military division of labor was simple, the levels of hierarchy few as well as rigidly defined, and within each stratum, specialization was almost nonexistent. The skill requirements were directly available in feudal society without additional specialized training. In particular, the aristocracy—the landed nobility—supplied the bulk of the necessary leadership, since their way of life prepared them for the requirements of warfare. Both family connection and common ideology ensured that military officers would form a cohesive group and would embody the ideology of the dominant groups in the social structure. Officership was not a specialized profession, but merely a part-time and occasional aspect of aristocratic existence. The officer even supplied his own weapons. The rank-and-file cadres were also drawn directly from their peacetime pursuits. Aside from small bands of mercenaries, soldiers came from the lower social strata where the appropriate skills for the few auxiliary weapons could be found. The role of warrior was a most honorable one and military status determined a person's prestige.

Because of the simple skill structure and relatively static organization, military authority was derived from tradition, custom, and social position. The aristocratic military establishment had an *ascriptive* system of authority. Authority was ascribed, in that persons were born into the officer class or they were excluded. Seldom could they earn such position through personal performance. The system of strict seniority, requiring promotion on the basis of age, is a keystone in the persistence of ascribed authority in modern armed forces. Age and length of service, like social status at birth, are ascribed group characteristics rather than marks of performance. The transforming of the aristocratic feudal military establishment into a professional armed force is linked to the growth of industrialism and the technological development of war. The traditional ascriptive basis of military authority becomes modified with a greater and greater reliance on criteria of *achievement* as the basis for allocating positions of authority. Performance in training, technical competence, and career records of the persons supplant birth, social connections, and inherited social status. The emergence of a professional army—that is, more specifically, a professional officer corps—was a slow and gradual transition with many interruptions and reversals. Although in the eighteenth century the signs were clearly discernible, one cannot speak of the emergence of a military profession until after 1800.

Huntington identifies three essential elements in military professionalism: expertise, responsibility, and corporateness.[2] Professional practitioners—as in law and medicine—as a result of prolonged and specialized training, acquire a technique that enables them to render a specialized service. But in addition to sharing a special skill acquired through training, a professional group develops a sense of group identity and a complex of institutions for internal self-administration. Self-administration implies the growth of a body of ethics and a code of practice.[3] The importance of ethics and responsibility in the professionalization of the military is a complex topic. In modern times the military officer can practice his profession only in the service of his government. He is both a professional and a civil servant.

Thus the emergence of professionalism means the emergence of a career service and the decline of the gentleman in warfare.[4] The aristocratic officer began to be displaced as artillery and more elaborate logistic planning required that the military be a trained and a full-time occupation. An upper-class education failed to provide the mathematical and engineering background that the occupation now required. Historical research highlights the evolution of the military profession as middle-class technicians during the nineteenth century took over the specialized artillery and engineering services, while the infantry and to an even greater extent the cavalry remained the domain of the aristocracy.[5] As the simple division of labor gave way to a complex pattern of specialization, the number of ranks increased and the staff officer emerged as a specialist in planning and coordination. The military became a profession in the employ of the state, separated by training from other professionals and dependent on the state for his complex instruments of warfare. All of these transformations implied that positions of authority would have to be allocated to persons with demonstrated competence, that is, on the basis of achievement.

The new skill structure of the military establishment is one in which specialization penetrates down the hierarchy into the formations assigned to combat. The concentration of persons engaged in purely military occupations is now a minority and even the combat occupations involve technical specialization. The transferability of skill to civilian occupations is extremely widespread. Top-ranking generals and admirals particularly have many nonmilitary functions to perform which involve general managerial skills. These long-term changes in the military establishment can be seen from an occupational analysis of enlisted personnel since the Civil War. Military types of occupations accounted for 93.2 per cent of the personnel in the Civil War, but after the Spanish-American War the civilian types of occupations began to predominate. By 1954, only 28.8 per cent of Army enlisted personnel were engaged in purely military occupations. The percentages are undoubtedly lower for both Navy and Air Force personnel.

TABLE 1. OCCUPATIONAL SPECIALIZATION IN ARMY ENLISTED PERSONNEL, CIVIL WAR TO 1954

Occupational group	Civil War	Spanish-American War	World War I	World War II	Korean Conflict	Year 1954
Civilian type						
Technical, scientific	0.2	0.5	3.7	10.1	10.7	14.5
Administrative, clerical	0.7	3.1	8.0	14.6	19.2	17.5
Skilled mechanics, maintenance, etc.	0.6	1.1	21.5	15.8	16.9	20.3
Service workers	2.4	6.5	12.5	9.7	11.5	10.4
Operative, laborers	2.9	2.2	20.2	13.6	8.6	8.4
Military type	93.2	86.6	34.1	36.2	33.1	28.8

SOURCE: *Report on Conditions of Military Service for the President's Commission on Veterans' Pensions*, Question IV (Nature of Military Duties), December 28, 1955.

However, vestiges of ascriptive status and authority in the form of seniority as a criterion of assignment and promotion remain to complicate the incorporation of new skill groups. The dilemmas of authority based on ascription versus achievement exist in all organizations. But it is a recurrent civilian perspective that the military establishment underemphasizes achievement in order to maintain traditional forms and the privileges of seniority. Thus, for example, the close link between age and rank in the military profession, particularly in naval organization, sets narrow limits within which skill is accorded positions of authority. In short, the hierarchical features of the military establishment strengthen the ascriptive sources of authority and compound the tasks of introducing new skill groups into the military structure.

Consequently, there exists a deep source of organizational strain in military organization because the authority structure does not articulate with its skill structure. In all three services—ground, air, and naval—the increased number and complexity of technical specialists operate under the formally prescribed lines of authority developed for the simpler units of the past century. The basic dilemma centers about the staff officer who, despite his expanded functions and specialized skills, is defined as subordinate to the commander. Originally, authority was vested solely in the commander, and the role of the staff officer was defined as that of an adviser to the commanding officer. The supremacy of the commander appeared essential in order that specialists might operate within their competence and that they be effectively coordinated. This type of organizational structure in which the staff officer was limited to the role of adviser may have worked adequately as long as the technology of warfare developed slowly, but with current complex technology it is a source of continuing strain.

As the division of labor becomes more complex and more specialized, the commander's dilemma becomes more pressing. Technological innovations have often been introduced into military organization by the development of specialized units, rather than by the incorporation of specialized personnel into existing units. Consequently, the task of coordinating skill groups has been passed increasingly to higher levels of command. The major unit commander is not equipped with sufficient technical knowledge to supervise or assess adequately the performance of these specialized units, and is compelled to depend more heavily on the advice of his staff. Nevertheless, the commander is held responsible for their performance by the principle of hierarchy and the formal rules of the organization. The military establishment seeks to prepare him for this dilemma by increased schooling, rotational assignments, and specialized instruction in the techniques of management.

However, in reality, the commander is forced to increase his reliance on staff officers to ensure the efficient performance of technical functions. The formal regulations within which commanders must operate adhere closely to the principle of hierarchy and the traditional "chain of command." Subordinate commanders may thus interpret staff supervision as advisory in nature. Consequently, conflicts in the use of authority are created.

The staff officer, as a technical specialist, must exert supervision over a technical function in a lower echelon without the support of formal regulations or the traditional chain of command. However, if he fails to accept the reality of his supervisory authority, and accepts regulations and tradition, he risks a charge of negligence in assisting the commander in executing his responsibilities.

The problem of the subordinate commander is complementary. If he permits direct intervention by the staff officer of a superior echelon, he must do so without the support of formal regulations. He also weakens his position in the chain of command (and often loses the support of his own staff officers) by an admission of inadequacy in the supervision of a technical function. But if he resists superior staff intervention, he risks the displeasure of the corresponding superior commander, whose concern is for performance rather than formal regulations. Frequently, the only solution to the dilemma is that the subordinate commander must reject the technical authority of superior staff levels and exercise supervision himself over a function of which he lacks adequate technical knowledge.

The discrepancy between command realities and formal regulations in a staff officer's role in the Air Force was explored in a study by Samuel Stouffer, Andrew Henry, and Edgar Borgatta.[6] They charted the opinions of 2,500 Air Force officers on the conditions under which they believed that a higher echelon staff officer should handle a problem "unofficially" in a lower echelon staff section by dealing directly with the lower-level staff officer, as contrasted with the approved approach of handling it through command channels.

The extent to which reliance on informal channels is an acceptable norm is revealed by the fact that an overwhelming majority (77 per cent) of the officers favored direct staff intervention in a maintenance or supply problem occurring for the first time. In short, in the normal course of events, informal and unofficial staff intervention would be used. Moreover, when the same problem (maintenance or supply) has arisen frequently, 35 per cent still felt that such staff channels should be utilized. A stronger test of the reliance on such practices was officer opinion concerning a problem which was described as "seriously affecting the primary mission." For so serious a problem, 31 per cent still contended that they would use staff channels if the problem occurred for the first time. The die-hard "out of channels" officer drops to a very small minority of 15 per cent, who would use staff channels if the problem is seriously affecting the mission and has already come up in the lower-staff echelon several times. As would be expected, regular officers were least disposed to report that they would use staff channels, the volunteer reserve officer more disposed, and the involuntary reserve officer the most disposed. However, the magnitude of these differences was not striking, indicating that the staff-command dilemma operates for all types of officer personnel and reflects the basic problem of a complex skill structure operating within the formal military hierarchy.

The skill structure is to some degree defined not only by actual technical requirements, but by the image of technological complexity which has been fostered by personnel agencies with a vested interest to upgrade skill titles by elaborate descriptions of specific functions which have at times actually been downgraded. For example, the basic infantry unit, the rifle company, has seven occupational specialties compared to three in World War II. However, four of these specialties apply to five men, one applies to five other men, and the remaining two (light weapons and heavy weapons infantrymen) apply to the other 168 men. Only one of these specialties represents an addition to the skill inventory of the rifle company of World War II or the Korean Conflict. The added occupational specialties simply represent skills that were not formally distinguished during World War II.

A similar phenomenon appears in Air Force personnel data. The apparent increase in the disproportion between flying and nonflying (support) personnel is not so much a result of an actual increase in support personnel as it is in a reduction of the size of the aircraft crew. As more skills are built into weaponry (such as navigation, bombardment, and gunnery), crew size is reduced without a corresponding increase in ground support except for maintenance.

THE RANK STRUCTURE

A second source of strain in the military establishment flows from the continuous effort to develop a system of ranks corresponding to the new complex skill structure. In theory, in tradition, and in image, the military rank system was a continuous pyramid with direct and clear-cut lines of authority from the top to the very bottom. Actually, it has been transformed into a "flask-like" shaped hierarchy.

The traditional rank distribution was a single broadly based pyramid. In the Army the largest number of men consisted of privates, all of whom performed a relatively standardized task—infantrymen directly engaging the enemy. The task of the foot soldier required only limited specialization, and it was a specialization without comparable skills in the larger society. The officer of the line with his specialized technical knowledge likewise had no counterparts in the larger society. The number of officers at the higher levels of command and coordination dropped off progressively and sharply, although the concentration of technical specialists increased. In such a hierarchy, the number of ranks could be small, and direct lines of authority could extend to the very bottom. Traditionally, the Navy had a similar rank system.

However, the proliferation of skills in modern military organization has been accompanied by an expansion of the middle ranks. The new rank structure now resembles two distributions, one for enlisted men[7] and another for the officer corps,[8] rather than a single pyramid. (See accompanying Tables 2 and 3.)

A diamond-shaped profile for enlisted personnel is sharp and pronounced in all the services except the Marines, where its combat mission permits more of a pyramid structure. Even in this service the bulging of the middle levels is very clear. Among the officer ranks, the Air Force structure has already been transformed in a diamond or rather flask-like shape, but the same trend of proliferation in the middle ranks is noted in the other services as well.

TABLE 2. GRADE DISTRIBUTION OF ENLISTED PERSONNEL OF U.S. ARMY AND AIR FORCE, 1935 TO 1962[a]

Rank (from high to low)	1935	1945	Army 1948	Air Force 1948	Army 1952	Air Force 1952	Army 1962	Air Force 1962
			(Percentages)					
E-9							.2	.5
E-8	.8						1.0	1.2
E-7	.9	1.5	5.0	6.8	3.0	5.3	4.0	5.2
E-6	1.3	2.9	5.1	6.1	5.4	6.4	8.4	9.4
E-5	3.6	8.3	10.3	13.4	11.4	15.0	14.6	20.2
E-4	9.4	14.3	14.8	16.4	22.6	18.8	21.5	19.9
E-3	9.0	20.9	19.4	18.4	28.5	21.3	24.4	22.8
E-2	25.5	29.8	28.2	27.8	20.4	26.9	11.7	17.9
E-1	49.5	22.3	17.3	11.2	8.6	6.4	14.1	3.0
Total	100.0	100.0	100.0	100.0	100.0	100.0	100.0	100.0

[a] Reproduced from Lang, Kurt E., "Technology and Career Management in the Military Establishment," in Janowitz, Morris, editor, *The New Military*. Russell Sage Foundation, New York, 1965, Table 15, p. 69.

SOURCES: 1935 data from Secretary of War, *Annual Report*, 1935.
1945 data from U.S. Army, Adjutant General's Office, cited in Stouffer, S. A., and others, *op. cit.*
1948, 1952, and 1962 data from Statistical Services Center, Office of Secretary of Defense. Percentages do not total 100 because of rounding.

TABLE 3. GRADE DISTRIBUTION OF ACTIVE DUTY MILITARY PERSONNEL, 1962[a]

Rank	Army	Navy	Air Force	Marine Corps
	(Percentages)			
Generals/Admirals	.5	.4	.3	.4
Colonels/Captains	4.9	5.9	3.6	3.9
Lt. Cols./Commanders	11.7	11.9	8.9	9.2
Majors/Lt. Commanders	16.6	18.2	22.0	15.2
Captains/Lieutenants	31.2	26.4	38.4	27.7
Lieutenants/Lts. (j.g.) and Ensigns	35.1	37.2	26.8	43.6
Total Officers	100.0	100.0	100.0	100.0

Rank	Army	Navy	Air Force	Marine Corps
E-9 .2 / E-8 1.0 / E-7 4.0 / E-6 8.4 / E-5 14.6 non-coms	28.2	.3 / 1.3 / 6.7 / 10.9 / 15.4 → 34.6	.5 / 1.2 / 5.2 / 9.4 / 20.2 → 36.5	.4 / 1.4 / 3.8 / 4.6 / 11.0 → 21.2

Non-coms (E-9 through E-5):

	Army	Navy	Air Force	Marine Corps
E-9	.2	.3	.5	.4
E-8	1.0	1.3	1.2	1.4
E-7 non-coms	4.0	6.7	5.2	3.8
E-6	8.4	10.9	9.4	4.6
E-5	14.6	15.4	20.2	11.0
(subtotal)	28.2	34.6	36.5	21.2
E-4	21.5	18 /	19.9	17.1
E-3	24.4	24.1	22.8	20.5
(subtotal)	45.9	42.8	42.7	37.6
E-2	11.7	17.4	17.9	23.0
E-1	14.1	5.2	3.0	18.3
(subtotal)	25.8	22.6	20.9	41.3
Total Enlisted Men	100.0	100.0	100.0	100.0

[a] Adapted from Lang, Kurt E., *op. cit.*, Table 16, p. 69.

SOURCE: Statistical Services Center, Office of Secretary of Defense, 1962.

The changed rank structure gives the impression of an inflation of rank. Thus an infantry regiment in 1939 had three master sergeants, pay grade E-7, then the top enlisted grade, all assigned to administrative positions in the regimental headquarters. In 1964 a single rifle company had four platoon sergeants at this pay grade, all of whom were actual combat leaders. In 1960 two new ranks were authorized to enlarge the apex of the enlisted hierarchy and thereby increase pay and career opportunities: First Sergeant, pay grade E-8; and Sergeant Major, pay grade E-9. Thus in the Army enlisted ranks have been expanded to include almost as many pay grades as authorized for officers (9 for enlisted men, 10 for officers). All but one of these enlisted ranks is now achievable within the company, rather than the regiment as formerly, indicating that the hierarchy is completed at a lower organizational level.

A similar trend is apparent in the rank structure of the officer corps. The Personnel Act of 1947, which authorized 51,000 active duty officers for the Army, made captain the most prevalent rank, and the number of second lieutenants approximately equal to that of majors. This proliferation in the middle officer ranks creates the image of a weakening of authority, since officers hold their rank not only on the basis of the number of subordinates they command, but also because of technical skills.

Such escalation of rank among officers and enlisted men, especially by an expansion of the middle strata, is a typical manifestation of organizations which have grown more complex and where achievement criteria weigh heavily in the allocation of authority. More is involved than an attempt to raise the income and prestige of the career soldier.

As a result, authority has not been so much weakened as transformed. Military authority now more often relates to lateral coordination and cooperation than to a vertical exercise of authority between higher and lower echelons. The task of the highest echelons is increasingly to maintain a suitable environment within which the middle strata of specialists can coordinate their efforts. Thus such a typical operation in the Korean Conflict as an infantry combat team being provided air support by carrier based planes, exemplifies the necessity for supplementing direct orders of a hierarchical type by complex and diffuse lateral coordination.

Personnel policies have sought to offset the apparent weakening of authority by creating separate hierarchies of commanders and of technical specialists. The objective has been an attempt to subordinate the specialist hierarchy to the chain of command. The distinction between line officer and specialist is most explicit in the Navy. This solution fails to recognize the basic problem: that the separate hierarchies must be reconciled rather than insulated. The increasing importance of engineering and weapons developments in the military establishment blurs the traditional distinction between the commander and the technical specialist. The crisis is most apparent in the Air Force where displacement of the "fighter" is proceeding more rapidly and more completely than in the Army or Navy.

However, the increased prominence of the specialist may have the most pervasive effect in the career perspective of the professional officer. Kurt Lang has pointed out:

> No longer are officers, by virtue of officer status, merely military professionals. The new nature of military service drastically alters the significance of being an officer. For many it is less a professional commitment than a phase in a longer occupational career.[9]

Thus the rank structure of the modern military establishment reflects the same fundamental problem apparent in its skill structure. Organizational boundaries are maintained by traditional patterns of hierarchical authority. Within the organization, however, the necessities of lateral coordination by a stable cadre of technical specialists has resulted in an expansion of the middle ranks of officers and enlisted men. The skill structure and rank structure tend to converge in reality, despite the format of the chain of command.

STATUS SYSTEMS

Sociological analysis has long recognized that status systems are required to regulate and control the tensions and conflicts generated by competition among differing systems of authority. Authority, ascribed or achieved, does not operate solely because of the ultimate sanctions that an officer can mobilize. Rather, in any organization, civilian or military, authority systems operate on a day-to-day basis or fail to operate because of the status— that is, the prestige and respect—the officers have. If authority is traditional and ascribed, status systems are likely to be fixed and clear-cut. There are no special problems when skilled specialists or individual men with outstanding combat records, despite low rank, are accorded higher prestige than officers with higher rank. However, when status and prestige are in sharp variation to the contributions a person renders to an organization, authority systems are certain to be subject to strain and tension.

The effectiveness of military authority is deeply conditioned by the status and prestige which civilian society accords the military profession. It is generally recognized that, despite public acclaim of individual military heroes, officership is a low-status profession. The results of a national sampling of opinion in 1955 placed the prestige of the officer in the armed services not only below the physician, scientist, college professor, and minister, but even below that of the public schoolteacher.[10] However, a comparison of the public prestige of the category "Captain in the Regular Army" in 1947 with that of 1963 shows a very slight increase.[11] The relative prestige of the Air Force and Navy was found to be above that of the Army and the Marine Corps, as measured by adult opinion as to which service they preferred for their sons. Yet one adult civilian in two felt that he would be pleased if his son took up a career in the military services. Interestingly enough, the less educated civilian holds both the military officer and the public servant in higher esteem than does the better educated.[12]

An adequate level of prestige, difficult though that may be to define, is required to maintain organizational effectiveness and to inhibit excessive personnel turnover. In addition, the relatively low prestige of the military in the eyes of civilians conditions the conception that the military profession holds of itself. The military takes over this civilian image, with the result that the military exhibits extreme status sensitivity. The concern with status of the military professional is to be traced not only to the hierarchical organization of the armed forces. The military behaves very much like any other minority or low-status group.

It is, therefore, not surprising that the military establishment has evolved an elaborate basis for according its limited supply of status and prestige to its own members. Most pervasive is the criterion which is applied universally through the services, the distinction between the officers and the enlisted men. The other universal distinctions are between regulars and reservists, line versus staff, combat versus noncombat, and the like. There are also more particular designations, such as veteran status of a particular campaign, membership in a high-status formation, or graduation from a service academy.

An effort was made by a University of North Carolina Air Force research group to study empirically status rivalries at selected Air Force bases.[13] On the whole, these research studies were mainly descriptive and did not analyze in detail the consequences of status rivalries on organizational behavior. They overlooked the positive influences that status systems have on initiative and incentives. Two of the collaborators, James D. Thompson and Richard L. Simpson, summarized their orientation with the hypothesis that "when members of a minority status class are concentrated in certain parts of a unit, especially in positions of authority, organizational stress is likely to develop." Social scientists will be required to develop a more comprehensive view of the nature and consequences of status rivalries in military systems.

A published study from this project by Raymond Mack underlines the observation, well known to every alert military commander, that flying in the Air Force has more prestige than decision-making at the lower echelons; that is, operational units outrank command units in prestige.[14] But this system of prestige does not extend throughout the entire hierarchy. Although a combat ideology pervades the highest echelons, the prestige of decision-making and planning increases, the higher the officer advances. Thus in their career development Air Force officers and officers in the other services must readjust their perspectives, often with great difficulty, to new professional requirements.

CHANGING MILITARY DISCIPLINE

The new skill and rank structure modifies military discipline as well as status. At first glance, the military establishment is a vast organization for technical and logistical operations and a preponderance of its personnel are engaged in administrative and housekeeping functions. But military authority, if it is to be effective, must strive to make combat units its organizational prototype, and the character of military organization can best be seen in combat units. In combat the maintenance of initiative has become a requirement of greater importance than the rigid enforcement of discipline. In the succinct formulation of S. L. A. Marshall, "The philosophy of discipline has adjusted to changing conditions. As more and more impact has gone into the hitting power of weapons, necessitating ever-widening deployments in the forces of battle, the quality of the initiative in the individual has become the most praised of the military virtues."[15]

In a sense, the military ideology of authoritarian discipline has always been tempered by the necessities of human nature. But the close order formations based on relatively low firepower could be dominated and controlled by direct and rigid discipline. However, since the development of the rifle bullet of more than a century ago, the social organization of combat units has been changing continuously so as to throw the individual fighter on his own and his primary group's resources. Despite the proliferation of military technology, all three services are dependent on the initiative of a very small percentage of the fighting personnel, who are willing to press the attack under all circumstances. The Air Force during World War II discovered that less than one per cent of its military pilots accounted roughly for 30 to 40 per cent of the enemy aircraft destroyed in the air.

In World War II and again in the Korean Conflict, the command problem in the ground forces centered on developing the ability of the infantry soldier to make the fullest use of his weapons. The infantry squad, the air crew, and the submarine complement, all have wide latitude for making decisions requiring energy and initiative. The reduction in the size of air crews, and increasing reliance on small naval vessels have fostered a similar effect in the Air Force and Navy. Even the proliferation of military technology has increased the commander's dependence on the cooperation of the isolated specialist in communications or surveillance systems. Consequently, there is greater organizational dependence on the willingness of the individual fighter and his primary group to operate in isolation from the larger unit. The increased firepower of modern weapons causes military forces— land, sea, and air—to be more dispersed, in order to reduce exposure to danger. Each unit becomes increasingly dependent on its own organizational impetus, once the battle has started. Thus the military establishment with its hierarchical structure, with its exacting requirements for coordination, and with its apparently high centralization of organizational power, must strive contrariwise to develop the broadest decentralization of initiative at the point of contact with the enemy. As the destructiveness of weapons systems increases, short of total destruction, the importance of initiative increases for the military formations that survive the initial exchange of hostilities.

The combat soldier, regardless of military arm, when committed to battle, is hardly the model of Max Weber's ideal bureaucrat following rigid rules and regulations. In certain respects he is the antithesis. The combat fighter is not routinized and self-contained. Rather, his role is one of constant improvisation, regardless of his service or weapon. Improvisation is the keynote of the individual fighter or combat group. The impact of battle destroys men, equipment, and organization that need constantly to be brought back into some form of unity through on-the-spot improvisation. In battle the planned division of labor breaks down with the occurrence of contingencies not anticipated by tactical doctrine. Persistent initiative and improvisation would, however, lead to a gradual dissipation of tactical units, unless the integrity of the larger organization was not periodically reinforced. Withdrawal to reserve locations provides opportunities for reaffirmation of the doctrine and values of the larger organization, reevaluation of improvised solutions, and realignment of personnel.

The technology of warfare is so complex that the coordination of a group of specialists cannot be guaranteed simply by authoritarian discipline. Members of a military group must recognize their greater mutual dependence on the technical proficiency of their team members than on the formal authority structure. The military organization dedicated to victory is forced to alter its techniques of training and indoctrination. Rather than developing automatic reaction to combat dangers, it requires a training program designed to teach men not only to count on instruction from superiors but also to exercise their own judgment about the best response to make when confronted with given types of danger. The very designation "combat team" exemplifies the goals of such indoctrination, since it emphasizes the positive contributions of each person regardless of rank. Thus the operational code of the Israeli forces in the Sinai campaign was, in effect, "when in doubt, attack"—an expression of sheer initiative.

Obviously, technology conditions these changing internal social relations in the military establishment. The morale and coordination of a complex group of specialists cannot rest simply on authoritarian discipline. The complexity of the machinery and the resultant social interdependence produce an important residue of organizational power for each participating member.

Thus the impact of technology has forced a shift in the practices of military authority. Military authority must shift from reliance on practices based on *domination* to a wider utilization of *manipulation*. Traditional or ascriptive authority relies heavily on domination, while manipulation is more appropriate for authority based on achievement. By domination we mean influencing a person's behavior by giving explicit instruction as to desired behavior without reference to the goals sought. Domination involves threats and negative sanctions rather than positive incentives. It tends to produce mechanical compliance. Manipulation involves influencing an individual's behavior less by giving explicit instructions and more by indirect techniques of group persuasion and by an emphasis on group goals. It describes the efforts of leadership when orders are issued and the reasons for them are given. The term "manipulation" unfortunately connotes devious and morally reprehensible techniques employed without the awareness of the person or group toward whom they are directed. While such a meaning is current, an alternative derivation is possible. Literally, manipulation is derived from *maniple*—a handful—and implies a high degree of individual attention. It is impossible to analyze modern institutions without reference to a concept descriptive of the techniques used to exert authority, such as manipulation, or some more socially acceptable equivalent. Manipulation involves positive incentives rather than physical threats; manipulation does retain the threat of exclusion from the group as a control. The indirect techniques of manipulation are designed to take into account the individual soldier's predispositions.

Indirect techniques of persuasion are used to create an environment in which the attainment of group goals is perceived by the members as being in their own interest as well as that of the organization. The primary concern of the higher echelon is on the attainment of the goals, rather than the procedures used. The primary group is exploited as a crucial source of motivation in the form of enhanced esteem among peers. Initiative and creative problem-solving are facilitated. This conception of authority is especially compatible with organizations in which there is a high degree of technological development. As more procedures are programed into automated weaponry, communications, and surveillance systems, the individual operator can retain many operations which are not specified by higher echelons. Thus superior echelons need to be more concerned with his continued sensitivity to the mission of the organization.

The goal of military authority, in ideal terms, is to create stable and purposeful involvement at each level in the hierarchy of ranks. When military leaders operate successfully, they make use of their organizational skills to produce effective participation. So it can be said, as older forms of domination become outmoded, effective participation becomes a new criterion for judging military authority. There is no clear-cut conceptual agreement even in idealized terms about the nature of such authority, but the problem is crucial for all types of hierarchical organization. Terms such as "participant authority" and "fraternal authority" have been offered, but the specific designation is not the basic issue.[16] It is, however, necessary to keep in mind that use of the term "democratic authority" by some social psychologists is both unfortunate and misleading. Democratic authority applies to political processes, especially to election contests, and serves little purpose in analyzing administrative and organizational behavior, especially military organization.

The military establishment, despite its hierarchical structure and legal code, presents a striking case of this shift from domination to increased reliance on manipulation or managerial authority. There are cyclical trends in military discipline but the important issue is that the shift toward managerial authority has been gradual and long term. The development of an operating doctrine to accommodate the military profession in the United States to these requirements began before World War I, but it was not until World War II that these trends were directly acknowledged. The transformation of military authority can be seen in every phase of organizational behavior—for example, the narrowing of the differences in privileges, status, and even uniforms of the enlisted man and the officer, the development of conference techniques of command from the smallest unit to the Joint Chiefs of Staff themselves, or the rewriting of military law into the new Uniform Code. Emphasis on manipulative control varies as between the services, depending on the rate and nature of technological change. The Air Force in some respects has gone the farthest in modification of its organizational behavior.

Yet the long-term outcome of the current transformation from an emphasis on domination to increased reliance on new forms of authority is problematic. It is abundantly clear that present forms are highly transitional. Since the shift in function of military authority is based on organizational requirements, it is not surprising that even armies of totalitarian political systems display these same features. The organizational effectiveness of the Wehrmacht was based on well-developed practices of manipulation and group cohesion, within the context of radical repression of extreme political and ideological deviation.

Indeed, the shift away from organizational discipline based on domination is a manifestation of all types of modern large-scale bureaucracies. However, because of the severity and uncertain nature of combat, the military has been forced to react more dramatically and extensively to the pressures for indirect rule. Since the new discipline must operate within a hierarchical structure and must serve the need for complicated coordinating mechanisms, the shift from domination to manipulation develops high levels of organizational strain and many unsolved dilemmas.

The contradictory interplay of practices designed to stimulate group initiative and those practices required for organizational coordination are again widespread in contemporary bureaucratic organizations. It can be argued that they are more extreme in military than in civilian organizations. Organizations can and do function effectively despite internal strain and dilemmas. But the military organization has special characteristics which complicate and disrupt the successful incorporation of authority based on indirect control, group decision, and other manipulative techniques. The dilemmas are deepened because of the systems of command and control that are required to manage atomic missile systems. In these organizational systems, the demands for human reliability are extremely high, and continuous initiative is required to guarantee that safety systems operate with complete effectiveness.

Devices for maintaining organization balance under conflicting requirements are slow to develop. Thus, for example, extensive training and expertise are required to develop a skilled officer cadre whose use of indirect techniques of leadership will be accepted by subordinates as valid and not merely as a sham. The gap between formal regulation and procedures and the informal realities of command is also especially great. This becomes a source of tension and confusion, since it is obvious and easily criticized. The wide difference between the official and the unofficial is perpetuated, since the realities of combat are passed on from one generation to the next by personal contacts, or informally, and not officially or explicitly.

Equally disruptive to orderly incorporation of indirect discipline is the ideological orientation of portions of the military elite. In the United States and elsewhere, the military elite holds a basic conservative ideological and political orientation and often is alarmed at, and misinterprets, the new requirements of military authority.[17] Segments of the military elite see the new requirements as potentially undermining the entire basis of authority and coordination and as barriers to decisions on the strategic level. Concern with technological change does not necessarily imply concern with organizational change. Such officers fail to see how manipulative techniques supply the basis for developing the necessary strong subleadership required to operate effectively within a well-managed and closely supervised military formation. In fact, they fail to see that indirect and manipulative control of a rank-and-file leadership based on positive group cohesion is essential to maintain both decentralized initiative and operational control over widely dispersed military formations. The "bruderschaft" of the Waffen SS represents an example of how such procedures can be developed within a very rigid command structure.

It is not necessary to assume that indirect social control implies an inability to arrive at strategic or tactical decisions. To the contrary, staff work in support of the strategic commander has traditionally assumed a range of interplay before the responsible authority arrives at a decision. The requirements of command have pushed this form of decision-making down to the lowest operational units. It is understandable that such a trend is resisted by military traditionalists. Military elites, typically, are concerned that indirect control should not undermine the basic authority structure and, therefore, feel repeatedly compelled, without clear criteria, to attempt to limit the use of group consensus procedures by lower commanders. Consequently, as the older techniques of military domination break down under technological requirements, newer forms based on manipulation emerge as highly unstable and loaded with tension. One formulation of the research task of sociologists is to study the strength versus the organizational vulnerability of contemporary military discipline. A functional analysis of changing military discipline requires an examination of at least three topics, which comprise the subject matter of the next chapters: the assimilation of military roles, primary group structure, and techniques of organizational control.

NOTES TO CHAPTER 2

1. Vagts, Alfred, *A History of Militarism*. W. W. Norton and Co., New York, 1937.

2. Huntington, Samuel P., *The Soldier and the State*. Harvard University Press, Cambridge, Mass., 1957, pp. 7–10.

3. Carr-Saunders, A. M., and P. A. Wilson, *The Professions*, Clarendon Press, Oxford, England, 1933; Henderson, L. J., "Physician and Patient as a Social System," *New England Journal of Medicine*, vol. 212, 1935, pp. 816–823; Parsons, Talcott, "The Professions and Social Structure," Chapter 8 of *Essays in Sociological Theory, Pure and Applied*, The Free Press, Glencoe, Ill., 1949.

4. Michael A. Lewis in his *England's Sea-Officers: The Story of the Naval Profession*, Allen and Unwin, Ltd., London, 1939, traces the historical development of the British naval officer. The author defines professionalism in the military exclusively in terms of career considerations: provisions for the continuous entry of young officers, system of training the young officer, regular employment of the trained officer, reasonable chances of the officer rising gradually in professional, financial, and social status, steady exodus at the upper end of the service, retirement.

5. Demeter, Karl, *Das Deutsche Heer und Seine Offiziere*. Verlag von Reimar Hobbing, Berlin, 1935.

6. This study by Samuel A. Stouffer, Andrew F. Henry, and Edgar F. Borgatta is an example of a military service, the U.S. Air Force, creating the conditions for a social scientific investigation of a basic aspect of its organizational behavior. The portions of this study dealing with staff-command role dilemma have not been published. The findings are available in Final Report of Contract AF33 (038)–12782–Staff Command conflicts and other sources of tension in relation to officer leadership and organizational effectiveness.

Lang, Kurt E., "Technology and Career Management in the Military Establishment" in Janowitz, Morris, editor, *The New Military: Changing Patterns of Organization*. Russell Sage Foundation, New York, 1965, Table 15, p. 69.

Lang, Kurt, E., *op. cit.*, Table 16, p. 69.

Ibid., p. 78.

10. Public Opinion Surveys, Inc., Princeton, N.J., *Attitudes of Adult Civilians Toward the Military Services as a Career*. Prepared for the Office of Armed Forces Information and Education, Department of Defense, Washington, 1955.

11. Hodge, Robert W., Paul M. Siegel, and Peter H. Rossi, "Occupational Prestige in the United States, 1925–63," *American Journal of Sociology*, vol. 70, November, 1964, pp. 286–302.

12. Janowitz, Morris, and Dell S. Wright, "The Prestige of Public Employment," *Public Administration Review*, vol. 16, Winter, 1956, pp. 15–21.

13. Air Force Base Project. Sponsored by Human Resources Research Institute, U.S. Air Force, and executed by the Institute for Research in Social Science, University of North Carolina, Chapel Hill. See particularly Mack, Raymond W., *Social Stratification on U.S. Air Force Bases*, Technical Report no. 4, Air Force Project, Institute for Research in Social Science, University of North Carolina, Chapel Hill, undated, p. 10; and Thompson, James D., and Richard L. Simpson, *Status Classes, Morale, and Performance in the United States Air Force*, Technical Report no. 6, October, 1952.

14. Mack, Raymond W., "The Prestige System of an Air Base: Squadron Rankings and Morale," *American Sociological Review*, vol. 19, June, 1954, pp. 281–287.

15. Marshall, S. L. A., *Men Against Fire*. William Morrow and Co., New York, 1947, p. 22.

16. Janowitz, Morris, "Changing Patterns of Organizational Authority: The Military Establishment," *Administrative Science Quarterly*, vol. 3, March, 1959, pp. 473–493.

17. Brown, C. S., *The Social Attitudes of American Generals, 1898–1940*. Unpublished doctoral dissertation, University of Wisconsin, 1951.

Chapter 3

ASSIMILATION OF MILITARY ROLES

FEW ORGANIZATIONS place as much emphasis on procedures for assimilating new members as does the military establishment. Assimilation involves the ongoing process of recruitment, selection, training, and career development. Not only must the new recruit, officer, or enlisted man learn a complex of technical skills. He is also expected to master an elaborate code of professional behavior and etiquette, since membership in the military means participation in an organizational community which regulates behavior both on and off the "job."[1] In the process of assimilation the recruit learns the roles, the required behaviors of his office, which he must perform regardless of his personal preferences. Whatever gratification and rewards military life may offer, military occupations are frequently hazardous, strenuous, and at times irksome. Assimilation of military roles requires strong positive motives if military tasks are to be performed with dispatch.

Since the specific tasks of the armed forces are constantly changing under the impact of technology, assimilation literally extends throughout the entire career of the professional soldier. Career advancement also means abandoning one type of military role—tactical leadership—for another, organizational leadership and command. This is a difficult process involving extensive retraining. In a period in which the military establishment is directed to deter total thermonuclear war, and yet the possibility of limited warfare is in the forefront of international relations, it is not an exaggeration to speak of the crisis in the mechanics of assimilating military roles. Personnel have to be recruited and trained for multiple roles and for roles about which there is neither agreement nor clarity.

Sociologists have a long-standing interest in analyzing the mechanics of assimilation, since it is through these processes that organizations demonstrate their viability. The sociological perspective toward the assimilation of new roles in the military highlights the linkage of a person's social behavior before and after initiation into the organization. Changes in military life and changes in the society from which the officer and the enlisted personnel come are closely linked. The professional soldier and the civilian soldier are both products of the same social system. It is a fundamental error to assume that the military establishment is some sort of self-contained organism which digests and assimilates foreign bodies. The orientation which the civilian society gives to recruits—officers and enlisted men—will either assist or retard their assimilation of military roles. The basic values of civilian society also help define the roles of the professional cadres who have the responsibility of training new personnel.

RECRUITMENT

What are the social dimensions of civilian life which assist or hinder recruits in assimilating military roles? Obviously, civilian orientations toward military service vary, depending upon whether recruitment is for a peacetime or a wartime establishment. In the continuing "cold war" period, the military is confronted with the difficulties of recruiting for an establishment which is neither peacetime nor wartime in the traditional sense. Since the end of the Korean Conflict, the selective service system has been required to fill the deficit of volunteers for the Army, while the Air Force and Navy attract a sufficient number of volunteers, as well as reservists, many of whom are responding to the pressures of selective service.

For the potential recruit, especially the volunteer, a positive attitude is based not only on the task of the armed forces but also on the fact that the military offers an adequate and respectable level of personal security. For the enlisted man seeking a professional career, it offers relatively promising possibilities. The strong regulations requiring nondiscriminatory practices—whether they be regional or racial-ethnic, or social class—have had the consequence of attracting the socially disadvantaged, especially lower-class persons with rural backgrounds, and Negroes who develop strong career commitments to the services. De Tocqueville already saw that for many enlisted men military life was an avenue for social advancement in a manner similar to particular civilian occupations.[2] For the potential professional officer not only does the military profession offer an opportunity for education and social mobility, but it is generally considered to be an occupation which stands in contrast to the many routine tasks of civilian life. It is a profession with a sense of mission and adventuresome experiences, especially those connected with travel.

The raising of the pay scale of the armed forces in 1958, as a result of the Cordiner Committee Report, was designed to enhance career opportunities in the military and thereby decrease personnel turnover. In the new pay scale there is a sharp weakening of the traditional principles of pay increases based on length of service and an effort to develop rewards on the basis of merit. The concept of proficiency pay for enlisted men, originally intended to retain "hard skill" electronics personnel, has been gradually extended to include almost all military occupations. It is doubtful whether the military profession, as a profession, can solve its personnel problems on the basis of incentive pay scales, important as this may be. In the long run the rewards of civilian industry are likely to be more attractive for the most highly skilled and most proficient. The attraction of the military service for the professional involves such factors as style of life, social status, sense of mission, and the importance of military honor.

However, a negative image of the military establishment in the American social structure stands as a powerful barrier to the recruitment of personnel. In a society in which individualism and personal gain are paramount virtues, it is understandable that some elements in the civilian population view the military career as an effort to "sell out" cheaply for economic security, despite low pay and limited prestige. In this view the free enterprise system is real and hard, so that the persons who are unable to withstand the rigors of competition seek escape into the military.

Enlisted men especially are viewed as placing individual security ahead of competitive achievement.[3] It is difficult to explain why the military establishment, which is an organization founded on the function of violence, which places a high evaluation upon masculinity and aggressiveness, and which, in effect, has many elements of career insecurity, should be selected by persons seeking to "escape" the realities of civilian life.

There is no evidence that contemporary military assignments are more secure or "safer" than most civilian occupations, although such an explanation may have had some relevance in the stable peacetime conditions prior to 1940. Moreover, such evidence as does exist indicates that the type of personality which seeks excessively to "prove" his masculinity in the military environment is represented by the "neurotic" recruit whose military behavior under stress is most likely to be highly unsatisfactory.[4] Or, as the authors of *The American Soldier* conclude, "Broadly, we can say that the evidence seems to show that a stable home background, a healthy childhood, good work habits in school and association with other boys and girls, including participation in sports, were assets for the young civilian who put on the uniform and tried to adjust to Army life." They believe that these characteristics might be held to be typical of "good" rather than "poor" adjustment to civilian society. On the other hand, they were negatively associated with the probability of going AWOL and with psychoneurotic breakdown.[5]

While it can be argued that the military services do not attract disproportionate concentrations of persons maladjusted to civilian occupational opportunities, such persons may still be pressured into military service by the civilian community as a kind of preparatory school for life, for "making a man" out of a recruit. In fact, many of the aspects of military life which are deprecated by civilian sentiments can at the same time be pointed to as reasons why civilian society believes the military can operate as a reformatory. The military establishment is an all-male culture which informally tolerates behavioral excesses to a greater degree than does mixed civilian society. The military provides a disciplined and predictable environment in which persons not able to utilize the freedom of civilian society can more readily adjust. The need for conformity in the military establishment is put forth in the interest of national security and in these terms can be more readily internalized.

As a result, young adolescents in the throes of intergenerational conflict and students without clear-cut goals are advised to join the services and "grow up." Near delinquents are often encouraged to join or are "paroled" into the armed forces. It is noteworthy that the armed forces are able to help certain of these deviant youths. Precise evidence exists that felons who were paroled to the armed forces during wartime had a much lower recidivism rate than those paroled to civilian life.[6]

Another fundamental barrier to the assimilation of recruits to the armed forces is the ambiguous perspective of American society toward distributing the risks of military service. In time of major war and during the contemporary period of international relations, conscription has been necessary to meet manpower requirements, and the system has been accepted because of recognized necessity. But for the selective service system to be effective it assumes public sentiments which insist on an equal distribution of risks. At the outbreak of World War II, public opinion in the United States was not characterized by hysterical pressure against "draft dodgers." In contrast to World War I, there were few counterparts to the white feathers, the painting of homes yellow, and the use of the epithet "slacker." Instead, there was a widespread acceptance of the decisions of selective service and the feeling that those not in uniform had sufficient reasons. Universal service was accepted as essential and the importance of an organized allocation of manpower was taken for granted.

After three decades of selective service, civilian perspectives no longer operate to assist assimilation of recruits into the armed forces. Overt opposition to the system, even political criticism of its injustices, is virtually absent. But even in the absence of adequate empirical studies, it is clear that there is widespread confusion about military manpower systems, deprecation of the administration of these programs, and a reluctance to serve. Already by May, 1952, during the Korean Conflict, 83 per cent of a cross-section sample of 2,975 university students were found by Cornell University social scientists to be essentially negative toward their military service obligations.[7]

When war is reduced to a potentiality rather than an immediate actuality, such perspectives are very likely to develop. Since the potential selectee tends to evaluate the threat to national security as one involving total war, he finds it difficult to believe that his limited personal contribution is of any relevance. Those who have served, while they may understand the relevance of basic training, report to their civilian contacts that after basic training most of their military experience seemed without point.

But from the point of view of military management, the issue is deeper. The reluctance to perform military service is a fundamental expression of the personal hedonism of contemporary society. The Cornell University study found that personal, rather than military or ideological, factors were at the root of negative attitudes toward being called into the military forces. These personal factors included disruption of plans, influence of friends and family, and feelings of relative deprivation.

The administration of the selective service system has come to condition perspectives in those who are selected, which handicap the military establishment. Few selectees believe that the system works to allocate manpower in a rational or just way. The pattern of deferments and exemptions, particularly for married men with dependents, and the fact that only a small proportion of each age group actually serves, are the basis for this resentment. Although not necessarily outspoken or articulate in criticism of the selective service procedures, many of these youths, who see no basis for their selection, develop powerful negativism toward military authority, which complicates their assimilation. These negative attitudes can be so deep that selectees succeed in communicating their hostility to the professional cadres and even adversely influence the outlook of junior officers.

Actually, since the outbreak of Korean hostilities, selective service probably operates to procure a relatively larger number of lower class youth for the Army. Although at the time of registration all social classes are represented, by the time of call-up for induction, lower class youths will be less likely to have acquired occupational or educational deferment. Health and mental achievement requirements operate in the opposite direction in that large numbers of lower class Negro youths are not selected. Induction and assignment policies ultimately influence the allocation of risk by social class. A. J. Mayer and T. F. Hoult, relating casualties to their place of residence in Detroit, concluded that the risks of combat were borne disproportionately by lower class men during the Korean Conflict.[8]

Selective service recruits have tended to be more mature than regular army enlistees. The relative maturity in age of selective service inductees accounts for their correspondingly better behavior in the military service.[9] For the volunteer into the Army, the sudden transition from high school to an environment of rigid surveillance has been conducive to strain and even delinquency. In general, studies of military delinquency consistently show that selectees are less frequently involved in misconduct leading to courts-martial or administrative discharge than are regular army men.[10]

Differentials in length of service between regular army and selective service personnel have also been a source of difficulty. The three-year term of service of the younger regular army soldier tends to be viewed as an employment contract with few penalties for failure to complete it successfully. However, the two-year term of the more mature selective service inductee is perceived as an obligation which he must complete successfully to maintain an established position in the civilian community to which he will return.

SELECTION AND TRAINING

Assimilation into the military establishment operates on the assumption that personnel selection procedures are able to locate those persons with the requisite mental, emotional and physical abilities for military training and service. As a result, the armed forces are deeply concerned with scientific screening devices, for within the broad range of general aptitudes, personnel with specific aptitudes for a wide variety of military tasks must be identified, including those with potentials for combat and combat leadership. In selecting for officer training, and especially for entrance into the service academies, the object is to screen for potential strategic leadership.

Psychiatric screening has become a more effective tool of military management by increased sensitivity to the organizational requirements for which the screening is performed. During World War II the unrealistic goal of predicting the probability of breakdown excluded large numbers from service and resulted in excessive rejections and a waste of scarce manpower resources. Eli Ginzberg and his associates have carefully documented the consequences and limitations of these screening devices.[11] Since World War II induction screening has increasingly sought to eliminate only the most grossly unfit. Primary emphasis has shifted to the basic training experience as a trial period of service where emotional capacity can be more adequately assessed. The development of the administrative discharge has facilitated the rapid elimination of persons with emotional and behavioral defects that could not be predicted prior to recruitment.

Classification and assignment techniques have become increasingly complex. The simple scores of general intelligence used during World War II have been replaced by more complex instruments. In the Army, the Army Classification Battery, a variety of aptitude tests, is employed to judge "aptitude areas" for various occupational fields. Such tests are administered at induction or enlistment and accordingly reflect exclusively the training or information that the recruit brings with him, rather than interests developed after a period of service. While such tests may have greater reliability, they often operate to impede the flexibility of personnel utilization by the immediate commander.

The apparent success of such tests stimulated attempts to develop similar instruments for the selection of combat personnel and leaders. However, after forty years of research and development in personnel selection, no satisfactory and reliable techniques have been developed. In part, the failure of personnel selection has been a theoretical one because personnel psychologists have sought to identify leadership as specific individual leadership traits when it is clear that leadership involves an interaction between personality attributes and social situations.

In 1947 W. O. Jenkins, in "A Review of Leadership Studies with Particular Reference to Military Problems," summarized the state of knowledge, as of the close of World War II.[12] He concluded that Morris Viteles' evaluation of leadership studies made in 1932 had not yet been modified. The record of accomplishment is not a brilliant one; no single trait or group of characteristics has been isolated, setting off the leader from the members of his group.

In a later summary which included post World War II efforts, Fillmore H. Sanford reasserted the same conclusion:

> Much effort, both scientific and otherwise, has been invested in the attempt to select young men who will turn out to be good military leaders. It is fair to say that, in contrast to the obvious success scored in recent years in the selection of people for various kinds of specific jobs, no one has yet devised a method of proven validity for selecting either military or non-military leaders.[13]

Past studies of tactical military leadership have also failed to consider the discrepancy between garrison and battlefield conditions. Formal psychological tests are peculiarly compatible with garrison conditions and stable assignments. The battlefield is, however, in many respects the antithesis of the garrison. The breakdown in the division of labor, an extensive range of contingencies, and the isolation of small combat units from command surveillance are almost impossible obstacles for the development of standardized criteria, or the validation of garrison measures in actual combat performance. There is, however, one conclusion from these trait studies which is highly relevant. Repeatedly, it has been found that academic and scholastic achievements are unrelated to tactical military leadership; this is neither a basis for selection nor for rejection.[14]

An elaborate effort to identify the traits of combat soldiers was made on personnel in Korea in 1953 after hostilities had terminated.[15] Known as the "Fighter Factor Study," it was conducted by the Human Resources Research Office and was based on interviews with 647 men in rifle squads. Of this group, 345 enlisted men were chosen by the research team as fighters or nonfighters on the basis of reports of their buddies and self reports on their behavior in combat. The subjects were selected by the research team to accentuate the differences between fighters and nonfighters. Subsequent psychological testing tended to confirm the original selections.

The results showed that factors such as better health and vitality, more intelligence, a great fund of military knowledge, and greater speed and accuracy on performance tests were found to be statistically more prevalent among fighters. The data suggest that fighters are more likely to be of middle class and nonfighters of lower class social origins. These variables would characterize active leadership regardless of the task at hand. However, the striking conclusion is that the degree of association was not pronounced. More fundamental from a theoretical point of view, the fighter was more masculine, more socially mature, had greater emotional stability and a more stable home life as compared with the nonfighter. Again, each factor by itself was hardly distinguishing in a crucial sense. However, if one thinks of the group requirements of combat, these traits become indices of a person's ability to participate in primary group organization under combat. Thus, for example, one of the most distinguishing characteristics was that the nonfighters came from homes in which the fathers had died before the son was eighteen years old. Such persons were deprived of the opportunity for identification with a male and for developing the capacity to participate in the all-male society of the military.

However, military organization is sufficiently diversified to accommodate some persons with mild or moderate psychiatric symptoms. Many positions involve isolation from peers. Personality mechanisms, enabling them to compensate for their lack of requisite social skills, may peculiarly equip some individuals for such positions. Thus a study of men who had taken a course of training as Navy frogmen found that the successful group (as compared to those who failed) showed more anxiety and talked less freely in the psychiatric interview, showed less creative ability and more depressive affect.[16]

In contrast to this tradition of searching for leadership traits, there has been a growing emphasis on a more sociological group process approach to understanding selection and leadership recruitment. Leadership, in this view, does not adhere to the individual, but is a varying relationship between personality and social situation. While this approach has proved valuable in the development of criteria for eliminating unfit personnel, again there is no reason to believe that selection procedures based on group processes are dramatically more valid and important.

The development of the group process approach to leadership selection received its impetus in the British army. The British had long resisted scientific selection, but after the crisis of Dunkerque, they faced the tasks of rationalizing their officer selection system and developed a program with great rapidity and thoroughness. The British selection system sought by quasi-experimental group situations to observe the behavior of men under stress and in leaderless situations in order to note which men would emerge as effective leaders.[17] Since these group experiments sought to reproduce some of the actual situations confronting tactical leadership, this approach is theoretically more relevant, although validation has not been extensive. These procedures were paralleled in the selection experiments of the Office of Strategic Services for its unconventional warfare operations. Unfortunately, the OSS research efforts, because they deal with such highly specialized personnel and because no attempts at validation were made, contributed little to the development of personnel selection in the U. S. armed forces.[18]

There are specific examples of the use of situational criterion measures, integrated into regular testing procedures. For example, in 1963 the U.S. Army Personnel Research Office established an Officer Evaluation Center at Fort McClellan, Alabama, which makes use of such procedures in a simulated Military Assistance Advisory Group setting. The delay in the development of this type of personnel selection is in part an expression of an individual psychological orientation and a lack of concern for the analysis of group processes. It is also an expression of resistance to the cumbersome techniques involved in group testing which require nonquantitative evaluations by the rating personnel.

However, the group approach to personnel selection in the United States has predominantly centered around sociometric testing procedures which, regardless of their validity, can be reduced to simple self-administered paper-and-pencil tests. These sociometric techniques for selecting leaders by nomination of peers, as well as by superiors, are usually built into training experiences, and become a mechanism for screening out persons with undesirable traits as colleagues. For example, the "Aptitude for Service Rating" used at the U. S. Military Academy, provides such a rank order score within each class which is a major component of the final class standing and consequently affects career progression.

Although validation studies of such techniques often tend to be fragmentary, there is evidence that student peer predictions are more accurate than ratings by superior officers, or academic achievement. A study of both officer candidate and West Point graduates in 1957 revealed that efficiency ratings in combat were more highly correlated with sociometric rankings while at school than with academic ratings.[19] It is important to note that the correlations between peer ratings at West Point and efficiency scores are highest for officers most recently graduated from the Academy, and decline as the officer's career progresses. As a result, the sociometric approach is criticized because it reflects popularity rather than the crucial social relations required to sustain groups under stress. At most, such measures reflect varying degrees of collegial compatibility, and this is clearly a relevant dimension.

The classification and selection of specialists for particular technical jobs, and even the selection of combat aviators during World War II and subsequently, is a markedly different problem from that of generalized military leadership. Aviators were not selected primarily as leaders; they were selected as aviators. It has been clearly demonstrated that old-fashioned selection boards did not succeed better in predicting who would survive aviation training than could be accomplished by flipping coins, and that scientifically devised selection tests did succeed in making such predictions with a resulting increase in efficiency. The improved selection of aviators as aviators leaves unanswered the question of how to develop leadership potential among these men who have been selected for a specific technical task. What is needed is a broadening of interest in research away from selection as a device to an understanding of the process of assimilation into the military, which involves not only selection but also the dynamics of training and career development.

Assimilation during initial training requires adapting the recruit to an all-male society and to a social organization committed to violence. The process begins with an effort to "strip" all of the novice's ties with the civilian world which conflict with the requirements of the military and to substitute new bases for identification. At the most personal level the recruit faces a loss of privacy and exposure to a pervasive set of controls. The initial stage of training stresses combat roles; thereafter there is a progressive specialization which recognizes that most personnel will ultimately perform administrative and technical activities.[20]

Training new recruits for combat has in the past been governed by a conception of shock treatment—of the need for a sudden and decisive break with civilian life and rapid exposure to the rigors of military existence. The officer candidate had to receive a double dosage of shock treatment, since he had to be separated not only from civilian society but also from the enlisted ranks. The devices of shock range from the "beast barracks" of West Point for new cadets to the well-known Marine haircut. The sharp and sudden transition is often repulsive to the civilian orientation. But, in the military establishment, the assumption is that only a decisive break is effective in the long run and that the rigors of basic training are in effect natural techniques of selection. Such initiation procedures are retained in the service academies, officer candidate schools, and aviation cadet classes, although they have been substantially modified in the basic training of enlisted men.

The shock technique was an essential element of the older forms of discipline based on domination. It probably had some functional utility. But with the development of military organization based on group consensus, the training procedures have had to be modified. It is clearly impossible for highly technical arms to achieve group consensus on the basis of negative sanctions. Instead, new ideals of assimilation stress positive attachments and group loyalties. While the residues of shock treatment persist, military training has become a more gradual process of assimilation. It is more a process of fostering positive incentives and group loyalties through a team concept. The training cadres—officers and enlisted men—must establish their competence and their interest in their men, for they cannot rely merely on their ultimate military authority and sanctions.

Hand-in-hand with the shock treatment, older forms of training placed emphasis on mechanical and repetitive drill, plus an overwhelming concern with the personal appearance of the individual recruit. With the change in training techniques toward the team concept, there has also been an effort to introduce the recruit to realistic military problems. The military establishment has not abandoned its tradition of "drill-type" training voluntarily and easily. In the ground forces the refashioning of training toward realistic problem-solving came gradually and as a result of failures of the older techniques in battle in World War II. In naval and air units, training by its very nature is more realistic, since every training mission presents genuine hazards.

The impact of basic training is carefully documented in a study by Richard Christie of 48 squads involved in the basic infantry training cycle at Fort Dix during the summer of 1952.[21] One of the effects of basic training was an improvement in the recruit's personal adjustment—as measured by his perception of himself as being in good physical and psychological condition—and in positive relations with his peers. Thus basic training did succeed in developing self-esteem and a sense of social solidarity among recruits. On the other hand, attitudes toward the institutional aspects of military life and of authority figures in the Army (officers and "noncoms") became more negative. In delineating the factors which assisted in adjustment to basic infantry training, the study revealed that recruits who remained in contact with their homes and family made the poorest adjustment to military training. Contact with home depended on whether the recruit's residence was close to the military base or at a greater distance. In short, the results give some support to aspects of the shock approach to training, so far as a clear separation from home is concerned. Furthermore, the structure of role relations in the squad could be modified to increase adjustment during basic training. Involvement of trainees in the leadership hierarchy on a rotation basis produced a strikingly more positive adjustment than those who had no such opportunity.

A suggestive study by Hanan Selvin demonstrates how leadership style influences the outcome of basic training, and indicates the potentials for creating a social climate appropriate for assimilating civilian recruits.[22] Using categories similar to the original Lewin-Lippitt-White group dynamics experiment, the investigator was able to identify three types of leadership at work in an infantry basic training installation which reflect the changes in military discipline. First, there was the arbitrary climate in which leadership operated by fear and with no admiration; second, there was the climate of the team concept—the persuasive climate—based on admiration for the leaders and without fear; and, finally, there was what was called a weak climate—the leaders were merely organizers and were neither arbitrary nor persuasive. Selvin found that positive identification with company leadership was most likely in the persuasive climate, much less in the weak climate, and least likely in the arbitrary climate. By investigating the leisure-time activities of the recruits, the researcher was able to observe how the arbitrary climate generated the highest levels of tension, so that the accumulated frustration of basic training had to be worked off in more violent, deviant, and extreme leisure-time activities.

As a result of the sheer pressure of organizational necessities, as well as self-critical thinking, training procedures have gradually moved toward an emphasis on group concepts and collective problem-solving. Military personnel do not succeed merely by habit, but rather because of their intelligence and adaptability. In problem-solving training the objective is to familiarize personnel with the environmental situation that they may have to face. Such training is designed to assimilate men into an organization where managerial techniques and authority are valid and effective. Once the recruit has mastered basic techniques, his unit is given simulated problems of actual battle conditions. Dress parade is replaced by fire demonstrations.

In theory and practice, these shifts do not imply that noncommissioned and commissioned officers seek to deny their formal position and official responsibilities. Excessive or sham display of social intimacy can be disruptive. One author is bold enough to speak of an "optimal social distance" for basic training.[23] Training cadres must demonstrate their interest in their men as well as technical competence.

However, the barriers to the development of functional training are immense. As in many aspects of instruction in modern society, the tasks of the teacher become more and more difficult to accomplish. Teachers must be more professionalized and more highly trained, but a lag in the upgrading of training personnel is often conspicuous in the military. In the past, the basic training center has been a low priority assignment which did little to advance the career prospects of the professional cadre. New policies have been developed by the services to improve the prestige and rewards of such assignments.

In addition, after the pressures of basic training are removed, garrison life again becomes predominant, and "spit and polish" measures are reactivated, often under the label of discipline. As a result, the recruit—often the potential career soldier—fails to develop a conception of a personal contribution to the organization's mission. As the armed forces come to depend increasingly on volunteers, the type of training offered will affect the type of personnel who will be attracted to the services. A professional military establishment which makes use of mechanical training procedures runs the risk of selecting personnel who will more readily conform rather than be concerned with initiative and problem-solving. The dynamics of assimilation during the training phase is a problem in the military establishment that lends itself to sociological research; the available empirical data are growing but still inadequate.

CAREER DEVELOPMENT

Since the skills and orientations which the new recruit—especially the officer candidate—is given during his initial assimilation are not necessarily appropriate for the later phases of his career, all services have developed extensive educational systems for retraining and for career development. Because combat is actually infrequent, the military establishment seems to expend much of its effort in training and retraining. In fact, the typical professional officer spends almost one-quarter of his career in school or in training situations.[24] The military educational system, especially at the intermediate and senior levels, has a dual function. First, by formal study and practical assignments, it assists the officer in adjusting to the organizational patterns of higher echelons. Social solidarity among officers who are at the same stage in their careers is established by intensive experiences as "students," in a difficult and crucial period. These "class" identifications persist as anchor points in their careers. Secondly, the school system performs a screening function. Competitive selection and relative class standings facilitate the early identification of some officers for accelerated career progression. For the organization this means facing the unpleasant fact that persons who were successful early in their careers may not show aptitudes for further career requirements.

The organizational dilemmas linked to career development form a basic theme of military life. The dominant role conflict is the conflict between tactical combat skills and the requirements of higher command. Although this is often described as a clash between staff and command, close examination of the military establishment seems to indicate that the dilemma is between differing leadership skills. In the command of small tactical units, techniques of direct control are paramount, and the display of technical competence basically important. In the organization of larger units, the elements of stress are more indirect and subtle and the techniques of leadership more complex. The military is no different from other institutions in that the higher the position, the less important specific technical skills are, and the more important are general interpersonal skills. Thus at high levels the skills of the staff officers and the commander have an important element of overlap, or at least foster a convergence of viewpoints between command and staff.

A different and less important dilemma in the career of the officer, especially in the middle ranks, is the role conflict between operational commander and teacher. A teaching assignment at the service academies is often considered an important step in career progression. The outstanding officer is given many opportunities for teaching, and teaching is often an excellent opportunity to develop skills required for higher administration. However, the shift from tactical unit command to teaching produces deep and often frustrating tensions which interfere with the officer's performance.[25]

The classical military solution to the dilemmas of career development has been to emphasize as much as possible the belief that the officer must be a generalist. Each of the services has developed a set of assumptions as to the components of an ideal military career and its educational system is geared to the development of this career line. Like all organization "myths," these assumptions are essentially correct in indicating the paths of advancement, but in many cases they can be inadequate in preparing personnel for emerging tasks. Therefore, career progression in the military is geared to attendance at a graduated series of schools, at designated points in the officer's career. Officer education develops through three levels: initial officer candidate training—in the service academies and at civilian universities; immediate command training—at the staff and command schools; and, finally, strategic training—at the war colleges of the different services or at the national war college. Throughout the structure are a variety of specialized and technical schools. A detailed description of the military educational system is presented by John W. Masland and Laurence I. Radway in a volume entitled *Soldiers and Scholars.*[26]

Since World War II officer education has been subject to criticism and has come under intensive self-scrutiny with the result that extensive changes have been introduced at the service academies. Officer instructors have been improved by sending them to civilian universities for advanced degrees, after an initial period of troop duty. The U. S. Naval Academy has a civilian academic dean and a majority of its instructors are civilian teachers. The number of elective courses offered in addition to the basic engineering curriculum has been vastly expanded, increasing the potential versatility of graduates. Social science courses, including sociology courses, are now offered at both West Point and the Air Force Academy. The academies have the dual mission of teaching the basic academic disciplines as well as providing a socialization experience for a professional career. The emphasis on indoctrination has often been interpreted as representing a narrow service orientation. However, Lovell concludes from his study of cadets at the U. S. Military Academy that "socialization at West Point produces only slight impact upon professional orientations and strategic perspectives of the cadets."

> During an Academy education, the cadet experiences only slight changes in his orientation toward his professional role and in the perspectives with which he views the use of force in international relations. Even more important, there is no single attitude pattern on these matters, either at the beginning or at the end of his four-year education. . . .[27]

The objective of the new curricula of the service academies may be described as an attempt to provide a general military education for early career requirements, and a foundation for prospective specialized training in military and civilian schools. A larger and larger proportion of professional officers do in fact go on to civilian graduate schools. The emphasis has shifted from preparing a standardized elite group to preparing an elite with a potential for versatility.

Similar developments have occurred at the more advanced service schools. There has been a marked infusion of civilian teachers and cross-service attendance has been stressed. Conference-type learning periods have supplanted formal lecture-recitation methods, while collaboration with civilian scholars in strategic and international studies has been greatly expanded.

Despite the emphasis of the system of higher military education on producing managerial leaders, there is a trend toward "specialism" in career development which contributes to an organizational cleavage between military technologists and military commanders. Specialists in transportation, electronics, or procurement tend to develop collegial solidarity that cuts across the conventional arrangements of the chain of command. Access to such opportunities, with no loss in promotion chances, is attractive to many officers early in their careers. Such a choice implies often advanced civilian graduate training and, consequently, enhanced post-retirement occupational opportunities.

Specialism poses a threat to military organization by reducing the number of officers available to assume command. Those best qualified to make sensitive judgments, and appraisals of complex situations, are frequently those most attracted to specialized graduate school. There is also an enhanced awareness of the hazards of command, and the fact that a specialist is less likely to make a serious mistake with long-range career implications. Thus only a commander can cause the failure of his unit's test by getting lost on a road march, locating his unit in the wrong bivouac area, or by calling for fire on the wrong target. The staff specialist can usually rectify his errors, or they are often concealed or balanced out by his colleagues.

Likewise, the distinction between academy graduates and others generates organizational cleavages. In the expanded military establishment since the end of World War II, the percentage of academy graduates who enter on duty as junior officers each year is only a very small number as compared with those from ROTC and other sources. For example, in 1957, of the 12,917 new officers who entered on duty into the Navy, 572 were academy graduates (approximately five per cent) while the concentration of military academy graduates in that year among new Army officers was even less, 406 out of 20,415. The basic fact is that all of the armed forces are obliged to make use of cadres of junior and middle level officers who are likely to have limited opportunities for advancement to the highest rank.

Academy graduates, marked for longer careers than other types of officers, pass rapidly through the command of smaller tactical units, and are more often provided with some form of technical training. The blocked opportunity for mobility creates problems of morale and tension. The consequences are most dramatically seen in the higher ranks, where elite positions are mainly reserved for the graduates of the military academies (see Table 4, General Officers of the U. S. Armed Forces, by Type of Military Education, 1951 and 1964). In fact, for both the Army and the Navy the concentration of academy graduates has increased from 1951 to 1964. The reliance on academy graduates is much heavier in the Navy than in the Army, and in both exclusion of nonacademy graduates from the top two ranks is complete. Only in the Air Force has there been an increase in nonacademy graduates at the general officer level, and this can be viewed as temporary in that the Air Force had a smaller cadre of academy graduates when it was organized. Thus while the armed forces display many characteristics of "civilianization," organizational autonomy has been maintained by the device of selecting academy graduates to the highest ranks.

Another crucial question that sociological research can raise about contemporary military education is whether it will produce future high-ranking officers who will have the point of view of a unified establishment rather than a more limited service perspective. Some light is thrown on this issue as the result of an investigation of a sample of higher officers (550) assigned to the Office of the Secretary of Defense, to the Joint Staff, and to each of the three service headquarters. The investigation was an outgrowth of the Henry, Masland, and Radway inquiry into military education.[28] On the basis of written answers supplied by these officers in a questionnaire, the ambiguous character of present orientations toward unification is apparent. The authors conclude: "The study indicates that officers assigned to the Joint Staff and to the Office of the Secretary of Defense share the 'broad non-service' values required in joint and national planning of defense policy."

TABLE 4. GENERAL OFFICERS OF THE U.S. ARMED FORCES, BY TYPE OF MILITARY EDUCATION, 1951 AND 1964

	1951				1964			
	Academy Graduates	Nonacademy Graduates	Total	(N)	Academy Graduates	Nonacademy Graduates	Total	(N)
Army								
General of the Army	75	25[a]	100	4	100	—	100	3
General	75	25[a]	100	4	100	—	100	11
Lieutenant General	61	39	100	18	95	5	100	40
Major General	38[b]	62[a]	100	145	78	22[a]	100	199[c]
Brigadier General	59[b]	42[a]	100	199	68	32	100	249[c]
Total				370				502
Navy								
Fleet Admiral	100	—	100	3	100	—	100	1
Admiral	100	—	100	5	100	—	100	7
Vice Admiral	100	—	100	21	100	—	100	31
Rear Admiral	80	20	100	220	87	13	100	252
Total				249				291
Air Force								
General	75	25	100	4	69	31	100	13
Lieutenant General	31	69	100	13	67	33	100	33
Major General	55	45	100	95	49	51	100	162[c]
Brigadier General	51	49	100	135	23	77	100	214[c]
Total				247				422

[a] Includes "Honor Schools" such as VMI and the Citadel.

[b] Includes one graduate of Annapolis.

[c] Based on 50 per cent sample.

SOURCES: Official Army Register, Adjutant General's Office, 1951 and 1964; Register of Commissioned Officers, Naval Personnel Bureau, 1951 and 1964; Air Force Register, Office of the Air Adjutant, 1951 and 1964.

They add quickly that "supporting institutional arrangemenis are not believed to be wholly in keeping with the required values." Broadly oriented officers are subject to a variety of informal pressures to represent the interests of their services and they are uncertain that their careers will be advanced since promotion rests with their individual services.

Career development in the armed services includes preparation for retirement and the transition to civilian employment. In the past, it was traditional for officers to serve for thirty years and to look forward to the pleasures of retirement in a warm climate, often in a location near a military installation. In the contemporary military establishment, twenty years of service is more typical, so that a second career for military personnel who retire at the average age of forty-five years is essential. They are likely to have on the average three dependents and therefore have pressing financial obligations.

The process of transition to civilian employment is facilitated by the skill structure of the military which now articulates more closely with that of civilian society. However, there are barriers to civilian employment of retired officers which are slowly being modified; for example, legal and administrative restrictions, negative civilian attitudes and lack of adequate information about employment opportunities. All of the services have started programs dealing with military retirement because of the growing magnitude of the problem. Albert Biderman has presented data which indicate that by 1979, one million persons will be on military retired status.[29] Over the long run, the ability of the military to recruit and retain superior talent depends in part on the success of military retired personnel in civilian economic and social life. It has long been recognized that for enlisted personnel, service in the armed forces, especially where the person acquires some technical skill, contributes to his economic earning capacity in civilian life. The observation has received substantial support from a study by Cutright of the effects of selective service on economic success.[30]

From the sociological point of view, the process of assimilation of personnel into the military is seen as a cycle involving recruitment, selection and allocation of personnel, training and retention, and finally preparation for a second career. The military personnel system is influenced by the new requirements of warfare in which the forces must be composed of highly trained personnel ready for immediate operations.[31] Citizen reservists must be organized on a stand-by basis. Short term, active duty officers will be more and more replaced by men who are available for periods of five to ten years of professional service. Longer and more continuous service will be required for enlisted personnel as well.

In meeting these organizational needs, the military services have displayed greater initiative and flexibility in dealing with recruitment than with retention of personnel. In particular, college ROTC, which supplies the bulk of officer recruits, has been more closely integrated with the civilian curriculum and academic life.[32] A scholarship program permits more effective competition with alternative civilian career opportunities. Two- and four-year programs have been authorized also in order to increase opportunities for recruitment.

There has been only limited exploration of the recommendation for a ten-year career as a technique of recruitment and retention of selected personnel. Instead the services have pushed to increase the size of the military academy and to train a larger proportion of regular officers who would be more committed to a full military career. Mayer Zald and William Simon's research on officer intention to leave the military establishment does indicate that academy-trained personnel have stronger career commitments than officers from other sources.[33] Of course, this is in part a result of the career opportunities they perceive. But, in fact, the armed forces depend heavily on developing a professional commitment among nonacademy officers who entered with the expectation only of meeting their obligated tour of duty. The research of Zald and Simon underlines the fact that the decision to remain in service, both by academy and nonacademy personnel, is strengthened if officers feel that their skills are effectively being used by the military establishment.[34] The decision to resign is as much a push from within the armed forces as a pull toward civilian life.

The possibility of a fully professional armed force without selective service becomes a possibility although arguments, both military and political, can be offered against such a development. It remains problematic whether manpower needs can be met without selective service. There are also profound questions in a democratic society as to whether the national defense establishment should be operated without a citizen component. However, it is clear that only a fraction of the young men available for service are needed by the armed forces, and therefore basic questions of equality of sacrifice are raised about the present arrangements.

An alternative concept to a volunteer armed force is a broadened conception of national service. Alternative paths would be available: military service, overseas and domestic peace corps duty, as well as a national youth corps for those needing specialized training and remedial programs in order to insure a greater equality of opportunity. Such national service could either be of two years' duration, or a scale of points such as was developed for demobilization in World War II and rotation in the Korean Conflict, could provide a workable and equitable formula for length of service.

NOTES TO CHAPTER 3

1. Janowitz, Morris, *The Professional Soldier: A Social and Political Portrait.* The Free Press, Glencoe, Ill., 1960, pp. 196–211.

2. De Tocqueville, Alexis, *Democracy in America*, edited by Philip Bradley. Alfred A. Knopf, Inc., New York, 1946, vol. 2, chaps. 22 and 23.
   Samuel Stouffer and others in *The American Soldier* (Princeton University Press, Princeton, N.J., 1949, vol. 1, pp. 314–315) report data on the pervasive extent to which social mobility and occupational training conditioned enlisted men's preference for branch of service.
   See also Eli Ginzberg's *The Negro Potential*, Columbia University Press, New York, 1956. This report concludes that the most spectacular increases in the opportunities of Negroes during the past generation have occurred in the armed forces.

3. Kluckhohn, Clyde, *American Culture and Military Life.* January, 1951, mimeographed.

4. Shils, Edward A., "The Contribution of the American Soldier to the Study of Primary Groups" in Merton, Robert, and Paul F. Lazarsfeld, *Studies in*

the Scope and Method of "The American Soldier." The Free Press, Glencoe, Ill., 1950, pp. 35–36.

5. Stouffer, Samuel A., and others, *op. cit.*, vol. 1, pp. 122–124, 144–145.

6. Mattick, Hans, *Parole to the Army:* A Research Report on Felons Paroled to the Army During World War II. Presented at the 87th Annual Congress of Corrections in Chicago, August, 1957.

7. Suchman, Edward A., Robin M. Williams, Jr., and Rose K. Goldsen, "Student Reaction to Impending Military Service," *American Sociological Review*, vol. 18, June, 1953, pp. 293–304.

8. Mayer, A. J., and T. F. Hoult, "Social Stratification and Combat Survival," *Social Forces*, vol. 34, December, 1955, pp. 155–159.

9. Ryan, F. J., *Relation of Performance to Social Background Factors of Army Inductees.* Catholic University Press, Washington, 1958.

10. Dubuisson, A. U., and W. A. Klieger, *Combat Performance of Enlisted Men with Disciplinary Records*, Technical Research Note 148, U.S. Army Personnel Research Office, Washington, 1964. See also Klieger, W. A., A. U. Dubuisson, and B. B. Sargent, *Correlates of Disciplinary Record in a Wide-Range Sample*, Technical Research Note 125, U.S. Army Personnel Research Office, Washington, 1962.

11. Ginzberg, Eli, and others, *The Ineffective Soldier: Lessons for Management and the Nation.* Columbia University Press, New York, 1959. Three volumes: (1) The Lost Divisions; (2) Breakdown and Recovery, (3) Patterns of Performance.

12. Jenkins, William O., "A Review of Leadership Studies with Particular Reference to Military Problems," *Psychological Bulletin*, vol. 44, January, 1947, pp. 54–77.

13. Sanford, Fillmore H., "Research on Military Leadership" in *Current Trends: Psychology in the World Emergency*, Stephen Collins Foster Memorial Lectures, Dept. of Psychology, University of Pittsburgh, University of Pittsburgh Press, 1952, pp. 20–21. See also C. L. Shartle's "Studies in Naval Leadership: Part I" in Guetzkow, Harold S., editor, *Groups, Leadership and Men*, Carnegie Press, Pittsburgh, 1951, pp. 119–133 (reissued in 1963 by Russell and Russell, Inc., New York), for a summary of the leadership studies conducted at Ohio State University.

14. This observation was first documented by research carried out during World War I by S. C. Kohs and K. W. Irle; see their "Prophesying Army Promotion," *Journal of Applied Psychology*, vol. 4, March, 1920, pp. 73–87. Literally dozens of studies have been repeated with little additional clarification of this complex issue.

15. Egbert, Robert L., and others, *Fighter I: An Analysis of Combat Fighters and Non-Fighters.* Technical Report no. 44, Human Resources Research Office, George Washington University, Washington, December, 1957, p. 68.

16. Heyder, D. W., and Wambach, H. S., "Sexuality and Affect in Frogmen," *Archives of General Psychiatry*, vol. 11, September, 1964, pp. 286–289.

17. Harris, Henry, *The Group Approach to Leadership-Testing.* Routledge and Kegan Paul, London, 1949.

18. U.S. Office of Strategic Services, Assessment Staff, *Assessment of Men.* Rinehart and Co., New York, 1948.

19. Personnel Research for Officer Candidate School. Technical Research Report 1107, U.S. Army Personnel Research Office, Washington, 1957.

20. Janowitz, Morris, *The Professional Soldier,* pp. 125–139.

21. Christie, Richard, *An Experimental Study of Modification in Factors Influencing Recruits' Adjustment to the Army.* Research Center for Human Relations, New York University, 1953, mimeographed.

22. Selvin, Hanan C., *The Effects of Leadership Climate on the Non-Duty Behavior of Army Trainees.* Unpublished doctoral dissertation, Columbia University, 1956.

23. Lammers, C. J., "Een sociologische analyse van de inlijving van groepen adspirant officieren in de zeemacht" in *Het Koninklijk Institut Voor de Marine.* University of Amsterdam, Amsterdam, 1963.

24. Janowitz, Morris, *The Professional Soldier,* pp. 139–149.

25. Getzels, J. W., and E. C. Guba, "Role and Role Conflict and Effectiveness: An Empirical Study," *American Sociological Review,* vol. 19, April, 1954, pp. 164–175. The teaching staffs at the Air University were the subject of this research.

26. Masland, John W., and Laurence I. Radway, *Soldiers and Scholars,* Princeton University Press, Princeton, N.J., 1957; see also Clark, Harold F., and Harold S. Sloan, *Classrooms in the Military,* Bureau of Publications, Teachers College, New York, 1964.

27. Lovell, John, "Professional Socialization of the West Point Cadet" in Janowitz, Morris, editor, *The New Military: Changing Patterns of Organization.* Russell Sage Foundation, New York, 1965, p. 120.

28. Henry, Andrew F., John W. Masland, and Laurence I. Radway, "Armed Forces Unification and the Pentagon Officer," *Public Administration Review,* vol. 15, Summer, 1955, pp. 173–180.

29. Biderman, Albert D., "Sequels to a Military Career: The Retired Military Professional" in Janowitz, Morris, editor, *The New Military,* pp. 287–336.

30. Cutright, Phillips, *A Pilot Study of Factors in Economic Success or Failure: Based on Selective Service and Social Security Records.* U.S. Dept. of Health, Education, and Welfare, Social Security Administration, Washington, June, 1964.

31. Janowitz, Morris, *The Professional Soldier,* p. 421.

32. Lyons, Gene M., and John W. Masland, *Education and Military Leadership: A Study of the ROTC.* Princeton University Press, Princeton, N.J., 1959.

33. Zald, Mayer, and William Simon, "Career Opportunities and Commitments Among Officers" in Janowitz, Morris, editor, *The New Military,* pp. 257–286.

34. *Ibid.,* p. 279.

Chapter 4

PRIMARY GROUPS
AND MILITARY EFFECTIVENESS

THE ASPECT OF MILITARY ORGANIZATION that has received the most attention from social scientists has been the role of primary groups in maintaining organizational effectiveness. By primary groups sociologists mean those small social groupings in which social behavior is governed by intimate face-to-face relations. During World War II many sociologists in the armed forces were impressed with the crucial contribution of cohesive primary group relations to morale, especially in situations of stress. Many of them discovered that, before their personal experience in military service, they had overemphasized the importance of ideological and political values in conditioning the effectiveness of military formations. Their experiences in the armed forces led them to discover or to rediscover primary groups in other complex organizations, such as the educational system, the factory, and the government agency.

The crucial role of satisfactory man-to-man relations in combat effectiveness was a universal observation during World War II. The eminent psychiatrists Roy R. Grinker and John P. Speigel summarized their work in the Air Force with this statement: "The men seem to be fighting more for someone than against somebody." Analysis of group cohesion of the Wehrmacht produced these two hypotheses among others:

1. It appears that a soldier's ability to resist is a function of the capacity of his immediate primary group (his squad or section) to avoid social disintegration. When the individual's immediate group, and its supporting formations, met his basic organic needs, offered him affection and esteem from both officers and comrades, supplied

him with a sense of power and adequately regulated his relations with authority, the element of self-concern in battle, which would lead to disruption of the effective functioning of his primary group, was minimized.

2. The capacity of the primary group to resist disintegration was dependent on the acceptance of political, ideological, and cultural symbols (all secondary symbols) only to the extent that these secondary symbols became directly associated with primary gratifications. . . .[1]

The trained combat observer and military historian S. L. A. Marshall states the same conclusion: "I hold it to be one of the simplest truths of war that the thing which enables an infantry soldier to keep going with his weapons is the near presence or the presumed presence of a comrade."

Yet it is necessary to bear in mind that cohesive primary groups do not just occur but are fashioned and developed by complex military institutions. At most, primary groups operate to impose standards of behavior—in garrison life and in combat— and to interpret the demands of military authority for the individual soldier. The goals and standards or norms that primary groups enforce are hardly self-generated; they arise from the larger military environment and from the surrounding civilian society. Consequently, the empirical study of primary groups must extend beyond the factors that contribute to social cohesion in the smallest tactical units.

Primary groups can be highly cohesive and yet impede the goals of military organization.[2] Cohesive primary groups contribute to organizational effectiveness only when the standards of behavior they enforce are articulated with the requirements of formal authority. The linkage of these elements—the norms of the larger society, military organization, and the effects of primary groups on combat behavior—is indicated by the problems of segregated Negro units during World War II. The norms of the larger society justifying occupational and residential segregation were assimilated in military manpower policies which assumed that unsegregated units could not develop intimate, primary group relationships. The assignment of personnel on the basis of such a group characteristic as race led to the development of primary groups with defensive norms, which were incompatible with the requirements of military organization. Primary group norms in segregated Negro units interpreted military authority as depreciating their personal dignity. The result was a wasteful use of critical manpower resources and the development of ineffective military units.

However, there is no basis in sociological theory to contend that segregated units uniformly weaken the effectiveness of the larger organization. An example in contrast to the experience with Negro units is that of the Japanese-American battalion of the Army in World War II. Widespread prejudice on the West Coast, and the relocation of their parents and families might have been expected to generate comparable defensive norms. Instead, they developed primary group standards which articulated effectively with the authority structure by requiring demonstrations of loyalty to the United States.

Nevertheless, the process of desegregation in the armed forces has been a dramatic achievement in military management, and a verification of sociological theory concerning social cohesion and organizational effectiveness. During World War II the Navy was the first to utilize Negroes in a limited number of combat assignments. During the closing phases of the campaign in Northwest Europe, a number of infantry companies had Negro platoons attached. Research on this experience indicates that it was successful, and should have dispelled the assumption of inherent differential capacities of Negroes for combat.[3] However, Negro regiments existed at the outset of the Korean Conflict, and full desegregation was not accomplished until the failure of segregated units was demonstrated a second time. Negroes were then assigned to combat units in proportion to their population in the larger society—limited to 10 per cent. One of the implications of this experience relevant to residential desegregation in the larger society is that the process is facilitated if a limitation is imposed on the concentration of Negroes assigned to a given area or unit. Under civilian political pressure, all racial identifications have now been removed and are prohibited from use in personnel actions or records.

SOCIAL COHESION

Social cohesion in primary groups, military or other, is affected by two sets of factors: the social background and personality of group members and the immediate social situation. In the military establishment common social background assists the members in developing intimate interpersonal relations; similarities in previous social experience such as social class, regional origin, or age supply a meaningful basis for responding to military life. From a personality standpoint, the ability to offer and to receive affection in an all-male society forms the basis of primary group solidarity. The social isolate is not a military asset and is likely to weaken social cohesion. A variety of studies, including *The American Soldier*, psychiatric observations, and the "Fighter Factor" study, seem to indicate that to some degree family stability, especially satisfactory identification with one's father, contributes to the ability to participate in primary groups. But this is only a partial statement, since it does not rule out the fact that strong emotions and even strong neurotic impulses may help a person mobilize himself to meet a military crisis. The capacity of personality to enter into intimate group relations in groups under stress is not well understood.

Moreover, it is not necessary to assume that cohesion in primary groups can only be the result of uniformity in personality or like-mindedness among its members. To the contrary, a division of labor and a blending of perspectives can be the basis of group cohesion. Likewise, from the point of view of the military establishment what may be crucial is that the members of the smallest tactical units have gone through some group experiences which demonstrate to them the value of social solidarity.

Thus along with social and psychological background factors, social cohesion of primary groups in the military derives from the organizational realities under which military personnel must operate. For example, this would include for each man: the technical aspects of his weapons, the type of organization of his unit and its replacement system, the nature of the military threat he has to face, and the performance of his immediate leaders.

First, the technical dimensions of the weapons systems impose limitations on stability and cohesiveness in military primary groups. Is the weapon fired as a team or is it fired by an individual? The increased importance of the primary group concept is an outgrowth of the trend in weapons which requires that more and more personnel operate technically as teams. Even the individual fighter has been outmoded in the infantry where the rifleman is trained to be a member of a "fire team."

Nevertheless, there is wide variation in the amount of communication and in the difficulty of communication between a closely knit submarine crew and a widely dispersed infantry unit. In some weapons systems it has been possible to develop a social definition of a tour of duty: 30 to 50 missions of a bomber crew. On the other hand, for the tank crew—in part, because of irregular commitment to combat—such a definition is impossible. Some weapons systems involve the aggressive expenditure of energy against a visible enemy, for example, the fighter pilot engaged in strafing. Others require only a mechanical routine against a distant target—for example, heavy artillery units. The amount of support a person receives from his primary group varies accordingly.

While generalizations in this area are most hazardous, it does seem that weapons systems which maintain close physical proximity of team members and enhance the process of communication contribute most to primary group cohesion. Moreover, weapons systems are accorded differential prestige in the military establishment, and the higher the prestige of the weapon the greater the contribution to group solidarity. The weapon becomes part of the self-image of the person, and the more powerful the weapon, the greater its contribution to the battle, and the greater is the person's sense of potency and group solidarity. Social cohesion in primary groups is not merely a human phenomenon; it is an outgrowth of environmental conditions, and in the military this means the technical dimensions of the various weapons systems.

Second, the type of unit organization, including the personnel replacement system of the U.S. military establishment, has certain consequences for group cohesion that are worthy of study. To the foreign observer, the American military establishment— and this includes all services—appears to be a "mass-produced" institution in which little effort is made to build on previous loyalties or to maintain organizational continuity. The replacement system stands at variance with many European military formations, which have in the past sought to draw their men from similar geographical locales or to maintain the identity of military formations. In the United States it is as if a democracy felt that randomization of assignment would ensure better distribution of risks and the destruction of units with military traditions would guarantee civilian supremacy. To some degree, this has been American policy.

Since World War I, in which units from specific geographical localities suffered disproportionately, military policy has tended to avoid geographical assignment. The competition of the services with the state-organized reserve system also tended in this direction. Absence of a desire for the preservation of traditional units within which to develop a stable and cohesive primary group structure is a reflection of the lack of concern with traditions in American society. But beyond this, it represents a technological orientation to problems of organizational effectiveness. While new machines are likely to be better than old ones, constantly disrupted organizations are not necessarily more conducive to satisfactory primary group relations.

One can argue that technical requirements of warfare have made geographically recruited units impossible and have rendered the preservation of traditional units most difficult. Nevertheless, the mass-produced character of the American military establishment is exaggerated in its replacement system, which tends to treat replacements as individual components rather than as group members.

When men do not know each other, combat units suffer in effectiveness. The loss of a single member can be most disruptive to an air crew; the new replacement must develop a sense of solidarity with his team. This is particularly the case in airborne units, with their high attrition rate. In a study of some 70 tactical episodes of operation Neptune, the airborne phase of the Normandy invasion, it was found that only a minor fraction was successful if the original unit was disrupted during the drop. If an officer or a noncommissioned officer collected a group of men he had never commanded and tried to lead them into battle, the results were almost uniformly unsatisfactory. The same observations were made from a study of battle stragglers in the Ardennes operation; individual stragglers had little combat value when put into a strange organization.

The observations of a young sociologist in the military service between 1954 and 1955 are most revealing of the disruption of primary groups in the course of basic and advanced training.

> Soon after basic training, the company is split up and groups of individuals are sent to separate stations. Even when a group from the basic training unit is sent to the same permanent station, before their army career is over it is highly probable that there will occur further transfers among them, thus atomizing the group which may have common memories and a certain amount of solidarity. The draftee sees other individuals being transferred from unit to unit. There develops an expectation that shifting station is a routine occurrence in the army. The draftee prepared himself for this by not involving himself more than necessary with any group to which he happens to be transferred. Any great psychological involvement with a single primary group, when a shift is possible at any moment, is very frustrating.[4]

Since weapons require teams of men rather than individuals, new forms of organization, replacement, and assignment practices have become essential. But a solution to these organizational problems is difficult to achieve. In World War II and in Korea, the individual soldier often had to be detached and removed from his training squad and sent to a line squad already in combat, where he had not had previous personal contacts. This practice was extensive during the period of the prolonged truce negotiations in Korea when individual replacements were required to implement the rotation system then in effect. Army regulations were revised to permit four "buddies" rather than individuals to be transferred.[5]

But the system of small group replacement has its built-in dilemmas and problems. Replacement needs within a company were seldom generated in the exact size of the packets. The arrival of a packet of four men, or of a replacement platoon, thus required the transfer of the surviving members of an existing integral unit to accommodate the integrity of the replacement unit. Consequently, as much unit integrity was destroyed as maintained. The arrangement also inhibited the commander's flexible utilization of replacements, resulting in discrepancies in strength from one unit to another.

There is a further theoretical consideration. Primary groups are by definition a system of informal interpersonal relationships. Their value lies precisely in their independence of formal organization. Consequently, replacement packets when assigned no longer constitute primary groups but rather an additional element of formal organization. Such solidarity as may develop can at times operate to the end of protecting the integrity of the packet from integration into the combat echelon. In another respect, the plight of the individual replacement may have been overstated. Studies have emphasized his apprehension about combat while in the replacement stream, but have stopped short of his ultimate integration into a combat unit.[6] Direct observations of this adjustment process indicate that infantry squads can develop informal mechanisms for receiving the replacement.

The greatest concern for organizational stability can be found in those units that are maintained in a constant state of alert for immediate commitment. In these units, replacements are more often handled as units, and there is greater emphasis on the movement of whole tactical formations as units. Increased mobility can make it possible to move whole units out of and back to home bases. The system of alert in the Strategic Air Command where each crew has a permanent continental base, is an example of a case in point.

In the contemporary establishment the maintenance of conditions required for primary group solidarity is yet to be achieved. Many units operate at less than full strength with a constant turnover of personnel. In all three services the return to civilian employment is considerable, especially at the junior officer level. In the air and naval units, the short-term reservist presents special problems in maintaining social cohesion. In the Army, where the two-year service for selectees operates, there is a constant rotation of personnel after basic training. Neither group nor individual replacements serve as a final solution. However, the importance of primary group cohesion has been recognized.

Third, social cohesion in primary groups is influenced by the proximity of danger and the importance of the mission which the group is assigned. Up to a point, as the threat of the danger increases and as the importance of the mission becomes apparent, the social cohesion of primary groups increases. This is the great difference between peacetime and wartime military establishments; this is the difference between garrison life and realistic training exercises, or between port duty and life with the fleet "in being." But what is the nature of the perceived threat in the cold war establishment, and how does a sense of mission influence social cohesion under conditions that require maintaining a state of alert, rather than responding to an actual military threat?

For the great bulk of the military establishment, organizational life is an eight to four-thirty job, with interruption for field training or administrative emergencies. Residence off the military establishment, the proximity of family, and the importance of civilian contacts dilute the sense of urgent military mission. In units on the alert, the function of the primary group is not only to prepare the individual for the pressures of combat but also to train him to withstand the tensions of maintaining a state of operational readiness.

Fourth, social cohesion in combat or under conditions of stress or extended alert depends on the performance of small unit leaders. For the contemporary military establishment with its emphasis on group consensus, tactical leadership must be based on example and demonstrated competence. As late as World War I, British officers carried the swagger stick as a ritualistic symbol of their command. Since their authority was based on social position and on direct domination, they had to demonstrate that they were different from the men whom they commanded. They would not carry weapons. They carried only a stick, yet they were able to get their men to fight. Today leaders must continuously demonstrate their fighting and technical ability in order that they may command without resort to arbitrary and ultimate sanctions. George Homans' analysis of "The Small Warship" illustrates how naval authority, despite its traditional basis, is also grounded in technical competence.[7] The military leader is a member of a team even after he has risen from tactical command. He must continue to demonstrate his fighter spirit; witness the Air Force generals who insist on flying their own planes, and the United Nations commander in Korea who carried two hand grenades.

The commander must recognize that latent subleadership resources exist within his unit, especially in the lowest tactical unit. His task is frequently that of establishing an environment in which such talents can emerge. This process is seen in a study of leadership in rifle squads by a research team from the Human Resources Research Office in Korea during the winter of 1952–1953. Detailed case descriptions of 69 rifle squads on the Korean front lines were collected, and platoon leaders and other platoon personnel contributed performance ratings of units under their commands.[8] Analysis of these data indicated that five "leadership functions" could be identified: (1) managing the squad; (2) defining rules and procedures for appropriate behavior; (3) performing as a model; (4) teaching squadmates; (5) sustaining squadmates with emotional support. The managing function occurred in virtually all squads, while the modeling, teaching, and sustaining functions each occurred in about one-third of the squads. The authors concluded that although the performance of these leadership functions was related to squad effectiveness, it did not matter whether the squad leader or some other member of the squad performed the function. Nearly one-third of the American members of the squads studied performed one or more of the leadership functions, and more than one-half of these were squad members other than squad leaders.

Combined with leadership by example, the military leader is required to display his interest and affection for his men. He must be interested in their physical and psychological well-being. He must share their discomforts in order not to weaken social cohesion with them. Such concerns border on intimacy, and traditional-minded officers are often fearful that social intimacy may involve an undermining of authority. In fact, social intimacy does run the risk of developing personal cliques which disrupt solidarity.[9] However, the irrational fear of intimacy creates a serious barrier to social cohesion. Morale then becomes mechanical and military formations lose their vitality. Consequently, with the breakdown of the older forms of domination, and the emergence of indirect controls, the question of the proper degree of intimacy between officers and enlisted men, and among enlisted men of different rank, becomes an area of ambiguity and stress.

These conflicts arise because tactical leaders must regulate the relations of their unit with higher authority. The commander is required by his men to defend them against arbitrary and unwarranted intrusion from above. Yet the officer in the tactical unit is also the final representative of coercive higher authority. For him to overidentify with his men would impair the system of authority. In the U.S. military establishment it is typically the senior noncommissioned officer on whom this role conflict devolves, and who has the task of adjudicating conflicting pressures. A suggestive study of the first sergeant in the Air Force highlights this process.[10] Squadron officers, it was found, tend to favor less authority or responsibility for first sergeants, while the first sergeants themselves and their subordinates favor more authority. In turn, the first sergeants would like to spend more time attending to the personal needs of airmen, and doing less paper work. By inference, junior officers would like to enhance their authority, but they are not prepared or permitted to display the direct contact with enlisted men that such increased authority would require.

GROUP BEHAVIOR UNDER STRESS

At some point continued exposure of any military group to stress begins to produce a weakening of primary group solidarity, and an undermining of organizational effectiveness. One of the direct manifestations of disintegration, which can be observed, is the nature and extent of psychiatric breakdowns. Every soldier has a greater probability of manifesting behavior of a neurotic or psychotic variety if subject to severe stress long enough.

The earliest explanations of combat noneffectiveness in World War II consisted of attempts to establish time limits in battle beyond which psychiatric breakdown was likely to occur. Such investigations were based primarily on the guilt-laden narratives of psychiatric casualties, far removed from their primary groups in combat. The shift in emphasis from individual tolerance for stress, to an understanding of the positive sustaining effects of the primary group, represents a major transformation in analysis and a corresponding shift in military personnel policies and procedures.

Because such estimates were based on data obtained exclusively from psychiatric casualties, intervening social factors, such as changing composition of the unit and its leadership, were not clearly identified. Peak effectiveness is reported to have been reached after three to five months of combat. After somewhere between 200 and 400 days of combat, the infantryman "wore out, either developing an acute incapacitating neurosis or else becoming hypersensitive to shell fire, so overly cautious and jittery that he was ineffective and demoralizing to the newer men."[11] The fact that this period of tolerance was twice as long in the British forces was attributed to their policy of more frequent intervals of rest than prevailed in American units.

The nature of the battle was also interpreted as affecting the incidence of psychiatric casualties. In general, the ratio it was assumed was one psychiatric casualty to four casualties who were wounded or killed. The rate was observed to drop off sharply in periods of full retreat or rapid advance. The explanation under these circumstances, in part, is that fewer casualties of all kinds occur, and consequently there is less disruption of primary groups within the larger organization.

The psychiatric rate also varied among branches of service and among different armed forces, as a careful review of research evidence on social environmental factors in military psychiatry by David G. Mandelbaum demonstrates.[12] There are very few psychiatric cases among United States submarine crews. To be sure, submarine crews are carefully selected, but since the stress of this service is extreme, social organizational factors, namely, the intimate organization of submarine life, must be operative.[13] A similar pattern held true for bomber crews in World War II, who developed tightly knit primary groups. In the Bomber Command of the RAF, for example, the casualty rate during World War II was reported at 64 per cent, including those who were killed, wounded, missing, and injured. Nevertheless, the psychiatric breakdown rate was only about 5 per cent.

Many observers have noted that the incidence of psychiatric breakdown among American soldiers was not only a reaction to the fear of being killed; often anxiety or guilt that was created over the fear of killing someone acted as the precipitating factor. Clearly, fundamental social taboos of civilian life were at work here. Psychiatric breakdown can also be delayed as a result of social factors. The most dramatic case was the low rate of neurotic behavior of the German civilian population under air attack, a rate which remained low until 1948 when deep-seated psychiatric symptoms began to appear as living conditions improved. The same delayed pattern was present among German prisoners of war, who had a lower rate than combat soldiers, but whose symptoms emerged after release from captivity. Thus it has been documented by research too extensive to survey that reactions to combat stress—as reflected by the incidence of psychiatric casualties—are influenced not only by the military situation but by social environmental and group factors as well.

At the beginning of World War II the concept of psychiatric breakdown had not been widely accepted in military organization. Psychiatric casualties were identified only by a simple diagnosis of "combat exhaustion" and evacuated from frontline units to avoid an implication of mental illness. The division psychiatrist was primarily a staff officer, and he functioned as a screening agent rather than attempting to provide treatment. Because of the press of battle, psychiatric casualties were usually evacuated to rear area field hospitals. As the distance and probability of reassignment to their original units appeared increasingly remote their group identifications weakened. Treatment at such echelons followed conventional psychiatric practice. The therapist, unfamiliar with the real combat situation, focused on the personality characteristics of the patient, and often felt impelled to promise relief from further combat duty. As a result, there were very few who resumed combat duty.

When the Korean Conflict began, psychiatric disease had become generally accepted in military organization. An improved diagnostic nomenclature enabled the psychiatric examiner to identify cases who could be helped by immediate intervention. Increased emphasis was placed on treatment of the psychiatric casualty within divisional medical facilities rather than evacuation to field hospitals. The continued proximity to his original unit, and the increased awareness of probable return to duty, sustained his group identifications. As a result of these factors, coupled with the changed nature of warfare in Korea, there was an apparent increase in the number of men returned to duty.

The rate of psychiatric breakdown is but one index of military group behavior under stress. It is one that has dominated thinking about primary groups under stress because of the abundance of impressionistic observations and the dramatic quality of psychiatric symptoms. But alternative frames of reference are necessary to encompass the dynamics of primary groups under extreme conditions. Another manifestation of the impact of stress is the tendency of combat platoons to develop a condition of wound sensitivity when confidence in success and in the supporting strength of the larger organization is lost. Under these conditions, there is an increase in the number of slightly wounded who abandon the battlefield despite their manifest ability to continue in the fight. As the bases for cohesion are lost, individual combatants turn increasingly to their own resources for survival. A similar phenomenon is described by Bruno Bettelheim, on the basis of his participant observation of human behavior in the extreme situation of the Nazi concentration camp, in the form of a process of identification with the aggressor—the process by which some inmates, in order to preserve a human identity, abandoned their own identity and assumed that of the guards who were persecuting them.[14]

Under stress of combat, as soon as a military formation encounters enemy resistance, long before the threat of psychiatric breakdown occurs, there is a tendency for interpersonal communications between group members to decrease and at times to break down temporarily. The task of the unit commander is to reestablish these communication networks. The fighter pilot on his first real mission feels completely isolated and his behavior may threaten his own formation. In the infantry, where group members are not physically held together as a submarine crew is, the group structure is strained under the impact of enemy firepower. The failure of a high proportion of infantry soldiers to use their weapons in combat is partly due to this breakdown of communications. The soldier is confronted by a strange situation in which he feels completely on his own. However, other factors are involved. One element is the possibility of exposure to additional danger and the norm of minimizing risk. Another is that he observes targets which are not comparable to the targets to which he has been conditioned to fire. Finally, there is the necessity for calculating the value of present targets as compared to possible future targets and the need to conserve an ammunition supply. Only when the combat group learns to behave as a team do its members become militarily useful. Realistic training, aggressive leadership, and mere survival through the initial onslaught, all of these help to overcome the disruptions due to stress.

The experiences in Korea corroborate the studies of World War II on the linkages of primary groups in combat with the larger military and social environment. For the enlisted men, and even for many officers, their perspectives were limited to their immediate tactical unit—the company and the squadron. Under the stress of battle, whenever there is a weakening of communications, the feeling develops that higher authority is acting capriciously and arbitrarily. The layers of military authority were remote and distant except for those few officers who had sustained contact with higher command. Civilian society penetrated into the daily life of combat personnel only by means of family contacts. Secondary symbols of ideology, even those of race and religion, were indeed faint while political concern was almost nonexistent.

However, in the more recent literature a new conception of primary groups under conditions of military stress has emerged. They are described as being more molecular or granular in structure, often a series of two-person systems rather than affiliations with larger numbers of men. However, this changed conception may be a result of more precise observations. Formulations derived from *The American Soldier*, based on attitude surveys, lacked an intimate analysis of the environmental and structural factors within the military unit. Older studies accepted a generic definition for the term "buddy." Three more recent and independent studies—in basic training, combat, and under severe environmental stress—have been conducted at a direct observational level where the dyadic nature of such primary groups could be clearly identified.

In a study of social adjustment in the basic training process, Marlowe describes the buddy relationship as "a conceptual precept that the individual seems to bring with him on his entrance into the service." Unlike friendship in civilian life, "buddyship" appears to be "an operational concept designed to take the place of friendship and serve as the initial stage in the potential foundation of a friendship." He continues:

> In the early stages of training, the importance of this kind of relationship is at times expressed with a vehemence. "Everybody has to have a buddy. Without a buddy you could never make it here." While such relationships often become intense, involving the pairing off of the individuals in almost all aspects of their work and off-duty hours, certain qualities attributed to friendship are usually verbally reserved in the trainee's analysis of the situation. The relationship is short-lived and will probably terminate with the end of the training cycle.[15]

Primary groups in combat are described in a study by Roger Little as a participant observer in an infantry rifle company during the Korean Conflict from November, 1952, through February, 1953.[16] During this period the main line of resistance had become stabilized and fighting was localized in bunkers and trench-like emplacements, and active hostilities were limited to patrols, occasional raids, and sporadic artillery and mortar barrages. Cold weather, barren living conditions, limited resources for diversion, and a long and threatening journey to the "chow line" operated as additional environmental stresses. The rotation system continually disrupted the stability of personnel assignments.

Under these special tactical conditions, a more elementary type of primary group structure developed than was described in World War II. The basic unit of cohesion was a two-man relationship rather than one that followed squad or platoon boundaries. Spatial dispersion and personnel rotation inhibited the development of more extensive interpersonal systems. The "buddy" relation was a cohesive unit built around the minimization of risk; a buddy was a person a soldier felt he could rely on in case of danger. The relationship was maintained as private knowledge; "one man could think of another as a buddy, but could never state it or boast of the attachment publicly." As a channel for the exchange of the most intimate communications, the relationship was a defense against isolation.

Similar observations were made by Richard Seaton in a study of military work groups under severe environmental stress in arctic Greenland. Although the threat of combat was absent, the conditions of life were remarkably comparable to those described by Roger Little as prevailing in infantry platoons in Korea. The form of social organization that emerged is equally comparable. The experimental group, subjected to prolonged periods of hunger "were more primitive and immature, and unable to sustain extended or sustained relationships." He concludes:

> With interaction resources very limited, men would reasonably choose to develop support relations with just one or two others rather than expose themselves to demands for reciprocity from all members; yet abstract valuation of all members might well remain high despite lack of interaction with them.[17]

At some point, just as individuals become prone to psychiatric breakdown, one can observe that combat units under stress begin to show signs of social disintegration if replacements and relief are not adequate. For many weapons systems, the unit is forced because of mechanical reasons to carry on their military duties; there is no other way out. But a pattern of military disintegration has been identified by sociologists which reflects the disruption of primary group life as a result of the breakdown of communications, loss of leadership, or prolonged breaks in the supply of food and medicine. The individual soldier becomes concerned with his survival at the expense of his military assignment. *Last ditch resistance*, which ends only with the exhaustion of fighting equipment and subsequent surrender or death, implies the absence of social disintegration. As disintegration sets in, resistance becomes *routine;* that is, orders are followed but resistance is discontinued when the enemy becomes overwhelmingly powerful and aggressive. Further disintegration under stress can lead to *passive surrender*, that is, token resistance by allowing capture after nominal face-saving gestures or by mere nonresistance.

Extreme forms of disintegration often underlie *active surrender*, the deliberate decision to give up to the enemy or to take steps to facilitate capture. Finally, *desertion* is an outgrowth of the most active form of social disintegration, since it usually involves the individual soldier breaking with his primary group and deliberately going over to the enemy lines. As Dr. Henry Dicks, a British psychiatrist, has demonstrated, the deserter may frequently be a person with marked neurotic symptoms. This continuum of organizational disintegration of military units is not necessarily related to the increased state of psychiatric malaise.[18] It is a response to stress in which the fate of the individual rather than that of the group becomes paramount.

In military operations against totalitarian powers, the maintenance of group cohesion even after combat is of crucial importance. As well as resistance to indoctrination after capture, escape, evasion, and survival emerge as serious problems when theaters of war spread over vast distances and uninhabitable territories. The political objectives of Communist powers require them to treat prisoners as potential recruits.

In Korea, American prisoners of war were subjected to extensive pressure to collaborate with the enemy. Shock to the pride of the American public was immense when it was reported that fellow Americans had turned "traitor" in Chinese prisoner-of-war camps. Although only a small number actually collaborated as a result of indoctrination, the belief developed that the Chinese Communists had perfected revolutionary techniques of indoctrination. More careful and more detached estimates, however, indicate that the techniques used were well known but had been applied with great intensity, although not always with great expertness or forethought.

Resistance to indoctrination after capture is supported by the persisting integrity of primary groups. Survival, escape, and evasion are often group activities in which cohesion may be a crucial determinant in the success or failure of the effort. Albert Biderman has stated in his *March to Calumny:*

> The passive resistance of almost all the POW's to the Chinese attempts at group indoctrination was a noteworthy display of group organization and discipline (although not always the traditional Army variety of organization or one that can easily be perceived by the more traditionalistic Army officers who are quoted in this book). The effectively organized resistance of the American prisoners to Chinese Communist attempts at compulsory indoctrination appears to have occasioned the abandonment of the efforts at forcible indoctrination in 1952, just as the resistance of the Americans earlier forced the Chinese to scrap much of their prisoner doctrine which had proved so effective when applied to Nationalist Chinese and Japanese prisoners.[19]

The variation in response to Communist pressure and indoctrination was extreme. The early captured ground force personnel who seemed to come from units that had not developed high social cohesion and who suffered extensive mistreatment after capture apparently supplied the bulk of the collaborators. The events of the Korean Conflict would indicate that the troops were not trained or prepared for the type of prisoner of war situation to which they were exposed. The defects in training were those that would have rendered them better soldiers, but it is problematic whether their resistance to Communist indoctrination would have been markedly different. Resistance in part was based on being a member of a military body and, therefore, the more effective the military body, the greater the potential for resistance. When membership in such an organization is severed or disrupted, the sources of resistance are also cut off.

This is underlined by the results of two carefully documented studies of the returned prisoners of war, which both conclude that there was a lack of correspondence between the extent to which prisoners were favorably impressed by the ideological doctrines of their captors and the degree to which they would go along with their captors in active collaboration.[20] Likewise, it is crucial to note that one of these studies by Albert Biderman on Air Force prisoners concludes that American characteristic tendencies, including a distrust of political dogma in general, and an aversion to Communist dogma in particular, formed a basis of their resistance to Communist indoctrination. While efforts to interview the prisoners for psychiatric and legal purposes have resulted in the accumulation of a considerable amount of evidence on how individual soldiers behaved under stress of Communist indoctrination, the dynamics of the social organization of the Communist prison camps have not been fully reported or analyzed. Because of the strategical background of the Korean Conflict, U.S. efforts to maintain contact and support for the captured military personnel were markedly limited as compared with World War II; these dimensions would also have to be covered for a full understanding of American behavior under stress. Thus, for example, there is reason to believe that among the ground forces there was a high concentration of personnel of lower and working class background. Therefore, their response, in part, to the political confrontation of the Chinese can be seen as a social class response.

Yet what relevance will the primary group concept have in years to come? Extrapolation from present trends may leave crucial questions unanswered. Limited or unconventional warfare requires increased reliance on the effectiveness of small groups, operating alone or in widely dispersed formations, over long periods of time, with limited support from the larger organization. But what about unlimited warfare, not in its unthinkable actuality, but in the prolonged preparation for deterring unlimited warfare? First, many combat units acting as agents of deterrence are not trained for prolonged combat but for single missions. What are the dynamics of social cohesion in such formations? The tension resulting from being continuously on the alert can be deep and pervasive. Second, many military units will be required to have both a limited warfare and an unlimited warfare mission. Is this technically and organizationally feasible, and what does this mean for social solidarity and primary group cohesion? The problem of group cohesion becomes even more complex as the military must relate its activities to formal and informal arrangements of arms control.

It is best for social scientists to assume that old concepts and theories still apply and then to be prepared to explore and discover what is new. Much thought will have to be given to the problem of social cohesion in units using new types of weapons, such as submarines designed to remain underseas for prolonged periods, or highly mobile infantry units equipped with low-yield atomic tactical weapons, or the like. While the current interest in the human problems of new weapons is mainly physiological, it will ultimately be necessary to discover and rediscover the social elements in these weapons systems.

NOTES TO CHAPTER 4

1. Shils, Edward A., and Morris Janowitz, "Cohesion and Disintegration in the Wehrmacht in World War II," *Public Opinion Quarterly*, vol. 12, Summer, 1948, pp. 280–315. See also Knut, Pipping, *Kompaniet Som Samhälle: Iakttagelser I Ett Finskt Fontforband, 1941–1944*, Abo Akademi, Abo, 1947 (The Social Life of a Machine Gun Company); an English summary is included.

2. A number of studies have been made of the dynamics of primary group relations in the armed forces without employing explicit criteria concerning the type of military behavior that primary group relations were supposed to produce. A typical example is R. L. Hall's "Social Influence on the Aircraft Commander's Role," *American Sociological Review*, vol. 20, June, 1955, pp. 292–299. These studies do not clarify the problems of organizational effectiveness.

3. Information and Education Division, Army Service Forces, U.S. War Department, Report no. B-157, 1945. Reprinted in Newcomb, Theodore

M., and Eugene Hartley, editors, *Readings in Social Psychology*, Henry Holt and Co., New York, 1947, pp. 542–546. See David G. Mandelbaum's *Soldier Groups and Negro Soldiers*, University of California Press, Berkeley, Calif., 1952, for an interpretive analysis of the problem.

4. Uyeki, Eugene S., "Sociology of the Cold War Army." Paper delivered at the 1958 meeting of the American Sociological Association in Seattle.

5. Chesler, David J., Niel J. Van Steenberg, and Joyce E. Brueckel, "Effect on Morale of Infantry Team Replacement and Individual Replacement Systems," *Sociometry*, vol. 18, December, 1955, pp. 587–597.

6. Merton, Robert K., and Alice S. Kitt, "Contributions to the Theory of Reference Group Behavior" in Merton, Robert K., and Paul F. Lazarsfeld, editors, *Studies in the Scope and Method of "The American Soldier."* The Free Press, Glencoe, Ill., 1950, pp. 40–105.

7. Homans, George C., "The Small Warship," *American Sociological Review*, vol. 11, June, 1946, pp. 294–300.

8. Clark, Rodney A., *Leadership in Rifle Squads on the Korean Front Line*. Technical Report no. 21, Human Research Unit no. 2, Fort Ord, Calif.

9. Simpson, Richard L., *Friendship Cliques in United States Air Force Wings*. Technical Report no. 3, Air Force Base Project, Institute for Research in Social Science, University of North Carolina, Chapel Hill, undated.

10. Karcher, E. Kenneth, Jr., *The First Sergeant in the United States Air Force*. Technical Report no. 7, Air Force Base Project, Institute for Research in Social Science, University of North Carolina, Chapel Hill, October, 1952.

11. Appel, John W., and Gilbert W. Bebe, "Preventive Psychiatry," *Journal of the American Medical Association*, 1946, vol. 131, p. 1470.

12. Mandelbaum, David G., "Psychiatry in Military Society," *Human Organization*, vol. 13, Fall, 1954, pp. 5–15; Winter, 1955, pp. 19–25.

13. National Research Council Committee on Undersea Warfare, *A Survey Report on Human Factors in Undersea Warfare*. Washington, 1949, p. 29. See especially chapter by Ernest A. Haggard, "Psychological Causes and Results of Stress," pp. 441–461.

14. Bettelheim, Bruno, "Individual and Mass Behavior in Extreme Situations," *Journal of Abnormal and Social Psychology*, vol. 36, October, 1943, pp. 417–452.

15. Marlowe, David H., "The Basic Training Process" in Artiss, Kenneth L., editor, *The Symptom as Communication in Schizophrenia*. Grune and Stratton, New York, 1959, pp. 75–98.

16. Little, Roger W., "Buddy Relations and Combat Role Performance" in Janowitz, Morris, editor, *The New Military*. Russell Sage Foundation, New York, 1965, pp. 194–224.

17. Seaton, Richard W., "Deterioration of Military Work Groups Under Deprivation Stress" in Janowitz, Morris, editor, *The New Military*, p. 244.

18. These categories of group disintegration can be compared with the categories of individual reaction used in the Human Resources Research Office study of nonfighters in Korea: (1) actively withdrawn or "drug out," (2)

withdrawn psychologically, (3) malingerers, (4) defensively overreacts, (5) becomes hysterically incapacitated. See Egbert, Robert L., and others, *Fighter I: An Analysis of Combat Fighters and Non-Fighters*, Technical Report no. 44, Human Resources Research Office, George Washington University, Washington, December, 1957, p. 14.

19. Biderman, Albert D., *March to Calumny*. Macmillan Co., New York, 1963, p. 43. This is a fundamental critique of the confused and contradictory reports of the behavior of American prisoners of war during the Korean Conflict, which is found to be comparable to prisoners of war of other nations and during other periods.

20. Biderman, Albert D., *Effects of Communist Indoctrination Attempts:* Some Comments Based on an Air Force Prisoners of War Study, Document no. 134247, Air Force Personnel and Training Research Center, Lackland Air Force Base, Texas, September, 1947; Segal, J., *Factors Related to the Collaboration and Resistance Behavior of U. S. Army PW's in Korea*, Technical Report no. 33, Human Resources Research Office, George Washington University, Washington, December, 1956. The lack of unification in the armed forces pervades social science research as can be seen by the fact that both the Army and the Air Force studied their returned prisoners of war independently, but research on this point did produce independent validation. See also special issue of *Journal of Social Issues*, vol. 13, no. 3, 1957, on "Brainwashing."

Chapter 5

TECHNIQUES OF ORGANIZATIONAL CONTROL

THE STYLE OF MILITARY ADMINISTRATION is to create a set of formal regulations and written directives which establish policy for all sorts of eventualities. The greater the imponderables and uncertainties that military command has to face, the more emphasis is placed on explicit orders, elaborate directives, and contingency plans.

First, military command structure is laid out and continually redesigned so as to create a precise format in which each unit is clearly charted and its tasks assigned. Organizational doctrine, although it varies from military service to military service, has its traditional objectives: direct lines of formal authority, explicit definition of missions, clear channels of official communication between staff and operating units, and limitations on the span of control.

Second, military command seeks to routinize its operating procedures to the most minute detail. Consequently, there are few remaining areas of organizational behavior which are not defined as official acts. The content of every sanction and reward is an official act. All the services publish manuals on staff procedures in multi-volumed compendia with never-ending supplements. This concern for reducing operating procedures to written directives creates the image of the military establishment as the most complete bureaucracy. The operating manuals of the American Telephone and Telegraph Company are no less detailed, but they do not encompass the vast range of topics that life in the military community entails. Operating procedures range from the making of a bed, the appropriate precautions for avoiding venereal disease, to safety measures for handling nuclear weapons in transport.

Yet it is obvious that organizational charts and rule books do not describe the way in which large-scale organizations operate. Informal practices and personal communication networks are required if coordination is to be accomplished. The military establishment is no exception. Much of the sociological literature on organizational control is taken up with the influence of informal organization. Often the assumption is made, although it remains to be adequately documented, that the gap between formal organization and informal realities is greater in the military than in other complex bureaucracies. There are too few systematic empirical studies of organizational control to permit generalization about the interaction between formal authority and informal communications in the military.[1] Nevertheless, common problems of communication in military systems have been often observed and identified by social scientists.

COMMUNICATIONS AND COMMAND CHANNELS

Sociologists agree that command channels and communication processes in the military establishment are not merely structural devices. Organizational control depends as much on what is communicated as on how it is communicated. Practitioners of administration and business management often tend to be concerned with "opening channels" of communication, regardless of policy content. Command channels and communications are effective or ineffective as a result of the policies that are transmitted. No amount of communication will overcome extreme differentials between enlisted men and officers, nor will the best techniques of communications compensate for a commander's lack of technical competence. In other terms, communications in a bureaucratic organization serve as facilitating mechanisms. Their effectiveness depends on the system of rewards and sanctions which has been created to develop socially cohesive units out of which an effective military system is constructed.

Command channels and communication processes in the military have their distinctive features. Like any large-scale organization, military command produces a downward flow of official and authoritative messages and instructions from the top to the bottom level. Yet informal messages flowing down from higher levels abound in the form of personal grapevines and deliberate informal prior notification of important decisions. One of the distinctive qualities of the military command channels is that these informal communications are required, since official communications tend to lag timewise behind organizational needs. These informal communications make it possible for personnel to prepare themselves and their units for new assignments and new tasks.

While informal downward channels are important to overcome time lags in official communications and command, the informal upward flow is even more crucial for effective organizational control. Military command has official procedures for maintaining an upward flow of information by means of reporting systems, technical chains of command, and official inspections. Nevertheless, the official flow of upward communication is less adequate than in some other types of bureaucracies. The military must rely on elaborate forms of informal communications to keep higher echelons informed. In part, this is due to the vast size of the military establishment and, in part, to the speed with which organizational developments need to be effected.

The informal and unofficial channels of communication are so important that they become institutionalized in the oral "briefing." At the highest levels of the Pentagon, one is struck by the heavy reliance on oral briefings, despite the military's concern with authoritative communications. The oral briefing is a rapid and flexible device for upward communications, which permits a more or less informal exchange of information. Since briefings are attended by many officials, they serve to bypass any single person who might bottleneck the upward flow of information. While the setting in which the briefing occurs is often one of studied informality, status relations can intrude so as to make it a more rigid channel of communication.

All organizations have hierarchical systems which impede the upward flow of communications and force reliance on informal communications. It is possible that military organization requires more elaborate devices for bypassing immediately higher authorities. The question also arises whether the procedures by which subordinates control access to the "old man" are sufficiently flexible to permit an informal upward flow of communications. The tendency in all organizations is to protect the chief executive from being unduly bothered; in the military, because formal rank and hierarchy is so clear-cut, informal access to higher-ups can be greatly reduced.

But again it is the possibility of combat, and not hierarchical organization, that produces the command and communications patterns found in the military. The business of the military is grave and deadly serious. Military control develops in an atmosphere where all directives tend to be expressed as authoritative and obligatory. Yet as the nature of modern warfare has become revolutionized, the traditional concepts of organizational control become outmoded. Just as the tactical commander must react to the dilemmas of his role and abandon traditional discipline, so higher echelons must develop new concepts of command. In order to coordinate complex operations, military command becomes tempered with military management—a concept that implies greater reliance on persuasion and negotiation. The tendency to resist these organizational changes in the military establishment is concentrated among officers in the middle ranks. At the bottom of the hierarchy, the realities of combat or training force leaders to adapt; at the very top, the pressures come from the outside and leaders are selected because of their inclination to innovate. But in the middle range, divorced from these pressures and often aware that their prospects of selection to the top are declining, officers are most likely to develop a defensive stance. Instead of constructive problem-solving, their concern with maintaining the formal prerogatives of rank leads to organizational rigidity, ceremonialism, and retreat from administrative responsibility.

The precision and schematic simplicity of military organization facilitate the introduction of automated communications and surveillance systems, and foster an impression of enhanced efficiency. Such innovations have additional results of critical sociological significance. In effect, electronic networks place great strain on human relationships. A centralization of decision-making at higher echelons is fostered by the relative ease with which problems can be referred to upper levels. Difficult problems are also transmitted with such speed that additional pressures are created for immediate decisions at the final echelon, often without adequate opportunity for consultation and reflection. The transmission process itself requires a simplification of the issue and, consequently, increasingly divorces the problem from the organizational realities in which it occurs.

These effects are now particularly apparent in personnel management policies. The introduction of automated record-keeping systems enables centralized agencies to distribute personnel according to explicit characteristics and presumed needs of a specific organization. At the same time, the local unit commander's ability to use with flexibility personnel assigned to him is inhibited. Fitness for assignment to a specific position will be determined by such abstract, reportable factors as test scores and service schools attended, rather than the commander's observation of the man on the job.[2] Vertical mobility is correspondingly retarded.

Such devices also complicate the processes of effective innovation and organizational change. Initially, the introduction of complex computer techniques requires major changes in staffs and procedures. Thereafter, however, the heavy investment in these devices and the extensive reorganization that their utilization involves, operate as impediments to further innovations which cannot be accommodated within the existing structure. Exaggerated reliability is attributed to technological operations with the result that conflicting human judgments are undervalued. Machines, like men, thus also resist change.

Computers and automated decision-making devices have been eagerly accepted by military traditionalists because they are peculiarly compatible with rigid hierarchical conceptions of military organization. Initially, it is believed that the larger the number of operations that can be programed into automated devices, the less salient would be considerations of motivation and morale as well as personal judgment. But such a result is hardly the outcome. More often the result is that a new range of decisions must be made by human agents who often do not believe that they have an adequate basis for making such decisions.

Organizational rigidity in the military establishment is most clearly manifested by the sporadic efforts to reinstitute traditional forms of organizational control when these forms are no longer effective. The requirements of international relations have prevented the military establishment from drifting away from a concern about the forms of discipline necessary for combat relations. The lessons of tactical initiative are best kept alive in those few units whose routine training most closely approximates actual combat or is hazardous. Nevertheless, the pressure to reestablish the discipline of the "old days" is continually present. Often leaders who see their particular weapons becoming obsolete, and who see no approach to regaining their organizational dominance, are the most ritualistic and compulsive about the older forms of military command; for example, the cavalry colonel in the interwar years, and more recently, even among aircraft carrier commanders.

This concern for traditional forms of discipline and officer prerogatives was stated in detail by the report of the Womble Committee of the Department of Defense, which in 1953 sought to investigate the professional status of officers after the Korean Conflict.[3] The report, written as a reaction to the reforms of the earlier Doolittle Board, not only dealt with basic matters of pay and promotion but expressed an emphasis on formalism which seemed to be more oriented toward ideology than to the realities of military life. The need for discipline and command based on domination has been emphasized in some quarters in the United States military establishment as an answer to the lack of realistic training and preparation of troops during the first phases of the Korean Conflict. However, in fact, realistic training that had little or nothing to do with formal discipline produced in Korea one of the most effective military forces in recent American history. The performance of military units in Korea is a striking

example of the conditions under which civilian apathy was prevented from influencing battle behavior by the performance of a
professional officer corps, especially the junior members, who
were convinced that their organizational integrity was at stake.

A return to organizational control based on domination can be
achieved only at a high cost. In a totalitarian society it can be
achieved because of the repressive political control that is available. Given the cultural traits of American society, the officer
corps runs the risk of losing its most creative intellects while the
noncommissioned ranks, as discipline becomes harsher, would
attract those who are unsuccessful in civilian life.[4] Any widespread and conscious effort to reimpose stricter discipline is
blocked by the political pressures available to selectees.

Since any serious return to rigid organizational controls and
discipline based on domination is blocked by the realities of
military life and by civilian pressures, nostalgia for the past
expresses itself in increased ceremonialism. The opportunities and
evidence for increased ceremonialism are ample—from the rein-
troduction of the dress sword for naval officers to more close order
military parades.

Ceremonialism can be functional if it contributes to a sense of
self-esteem and to solidarity. From a social psychological point of
view ceremonialism is among other things a device for dealing
with the fear of insecurity. But at what point does ceremonialism
interfere with realistic requirements? Much of the ceremony
seems to be a device for avoiding concern with the unsolved
problems of military management.

ROLE CONFLICTS

Organizational control in the military establishment extends
beyond command channels and internal communications. Every
soldier has other roles which can potentially weaken his ability to
perform his military obligations. The management of these role
conflicts in order to keep them in bounds has become a major
effort of the military establishment. The attraction of an alternative civilian career, the obligations of family, and the cross

pressures generated by civilian community contacts are at the root of these role conflicts. Compared with the military profession at the turn of the century, there is every reason to assume that such role conflicts are now more disruptive. A small, homogeneous, isolated professional group is less likely to be subjected to role conflicts. The civilianization of the military, as well as the growth in the size of the military establishment, weakens organizational control over the individual enlisted man and officer.

First, the revolution in military technology has increased the transferability of skills between military and civilian employment.[5] Even those personnel who have no specific technical skill may acquire general managerial experience in military organization which is more applicable to civilian occupations now than it was a half-century ago. Advanced training at civilian universities is frequently a critical point in career continuity. The acquisition of civilian occupational skills occurs at a time when the officer is in residence in the civilian community, and is exposed to frequent suggestions of alternative career opportunities. The numerous links between military activities and civilian business organizations, in procurement and research, create other situations in which essential contacts can be made.

As a result, military personnel has greater opportunity to shift from its military attachments to civilian enterprise, and organizational control is thereby weakened. There has always been a steady movement of personnel out of the military establishment. Among military academy graduates, comparable statistics on resignations show a gradual increase in recent decades. The professional soldier is also more aware of the possibilities of transfer and is more likely to consider and to reconsider the possibility at various points in his career.

Second, family responsibilities also create role conflicts. Military life involves routine transfers from one installation to another. The anticipated disruption of family life is another critical point in career continuity because it exaggerates the contrast between residential stability in civilian and military life. The shifting of assignments is also a feature of large-scale civilian enterprise. But in military organization, transfers are more frequent, involve personal expenses, and are often associated with a separation from the father for prolonged periods or uncertainty as to the availability of adequate housing at the destination. Especially acute problems in family life occur in units constantly on the alert and under strenuous training assignments. The effects of role conflicts among the crews in the Strategic Air Command were reported by Ruth Lindquist in *Marriage and Family Life of Officers and Airmen in a Strategic Air Command Wing*.[6] The strains of training and sudden overseas assignments generated family tensions that affected operational readiness and became a source of concern to Air Force commanders.

In the past, garrison life meant an intermingling of place of residence and place of work, especially during peacetime.[7] The military community had a strong sense of social solidarity and offered extensive mutual assistance to its member families. While garrison life may have isolated the military from civilian influences, it was a device for coping with the role conflicts and tensions that the military family had to face. But, as the military becomes intermingled with civilian, garrison life changes. Even among the Air Force operational units, the shortage of base housing is so great that many families live in the civilian community. The civilian community is not sensitized to the needs of military families and to their special problems. An increasing number of personnel are assigned to small detachments at radar posts or missile sites which are too small to justify the usual support facilities of a larger post, such as medical care, commissaries, post exchanges, or government housing.

For the military family, life in the civilian community creates many problems. As temporary residents, and usually tenants, they are often subject to economic exploitation. Their unique experiences and relatively esoteric way of life is in sharp contrast to their civilian neighbors. The educational experience of the children is a succession of schools of uneven quality, often contributing to apathy and retardation in the classroom. Living in two worlds, the military family tends to compare its lot with that of the civilian neighbor, often resulting in a sense of dissatisfaction on the part of the military wife.

Traditions of social visiting facilitate the adjustment of families of married officers. The task of adjustment is often more difficult for enlisted families because they lack a comparable tradition of social contacts within their status group. Thus in a study of the role of the Air Force first sergeant, one of the conflicting elements was the ambiguity associated with the social duties of the wife and whether she should originate social contacts among the other enlisted personnel in her husband's squadron. The civilian community offers few attractions for the unmarried personnel, except in commercial amusements and casual acquaintanceships of the briefest duration.[8]

These role conflicts, especially the conflict between military occupation and the attraction of civilian opportunities, are a primary factor in the turnover of military personnel. As would be expected, the turnover is greatest where the skill is more nearly equivalent to that in civilian employment—noncommissioned officers with electronic specialties.[9] In fact, according to a detailed personnel survey completed for the armed forces by McKinsey and Company, in September, 1956, the average rate of turnover of personnel in the military establishment is no higher than for industry, except in this one category. Turnover, resulting from role conflicts, is simply more disruptive to an organization which requires such high levels of social cohesion.

The military establishment has reacted to the competing attractiveness of the civilian community by attempting to restore many of the elements contributing to the solidarity of the traditional garrison. Indeed striking is the extent to which the military establishment has many of the features of a welfare state, without which these role conflicts would become most disruptive. While private commercial interests are continually criticizing the military for its post exchanges and for its welfare services, these features are important sources of institutional control. The social services once provided informally now operate on an organized basis, often with professional social workers. The Army Medical Service and the Dependent Aid Program of the Air Force use teams of specialists to prevent family disruption. The real value of military medical facilities, post exchanges, commissaries, and clubs is social rather than monetary. They provide a standardized and familiar environment at successive stations for an occupational group without enduring bonds to a specific local community. Such facilities also provide a setting for social intercourse based on a common experience in service life. Recurrent complaints of military leaders that "fringe benefits are being whittled away" frequently express a concern that their capability for maintaining this solidarity of the military community is being reduced.

The chaplain and the psychiatrist, with their loose relationship to the channels of command, have the task of reducing by indirect and "therapeutic" techniques the role conflicts of military life. Both have larger roles, however, in shaping military personnel policy, based largely on their high prestige in the larger society. The psychiatrist has become an important arbiter of what constitutes appropriate behavior and how defiant behavior will be managed.[10] Through the mechanism of the administrative discharge, delinquency, antisocial behavior, and nonconformity have become regarded as psychiatric issues as well as problems in military law. Since the base of their prestige is in the larger society—although they function as military officers—it is frequently possible for them to circumvent and modify military authority, or to reinforce military personnel policy with the sanction of medical science. From a suggestive study of the "Role Conflicts of Military Chaplains" by Waldo W. Burchard,[11] the inference can be drawn that the chaplain in his role as "social worker" is not so effective as the psychiatrist. Often he overidentifies or completely accepts the official military perspective and has a smaller sphere of independent influence.

INDOCTRINATION

Organizational control also requires indoctrination of military personnel. Current indoctrination programs include three quite different elements: (1) the professional code of military behavior; (2) the strategic concepts of existing or prospective military operations including a description of the enemy; and (3) the political objectives of U.S. national security policy. For the professional officer, a sense of honor is in itself a powerful ideological factor in organizational control in the armed forces.[12] However, since it is traditional to assume that the armed forces should be nonpolitical in a democracy, efforts to develop an ideological concept of the military mission have met with little success and have perhaps been a source of confusion.

The military forces of the United States had their origins in a revolutionary political movement—in an anticolonial struggle—yet their professional code of behavior is derived from the aristocratic forms against which they struggled. Among the basic elements of this code are dedicated patriotism, an almost mystical allegiance to the national identity, political conservatism, and a sense of personal fealty to the chief sovereign—the president instead of king. The professional code of the military is now compatible with technical training and expertise, but, basically, it prepares the soldier for a "heroic career" and not merely for a specific technical occupation.[13]

Although the professional code of the military arose out of aristocratic traditions of fealty, it has had to modify its symbolic content. The professional code of the military is, so to speak, a self-generating one seeking to draw inspiration from its own historical achievements, its religious devotion, and its sense of fraternity. For these purposes, military history is not reality; it is not the account of personal rivalries among competing generals, nor the account of the failures of the War of 1812 or the Spanish-American War, although the armed forces study these errors. It is an interpretation of past events designed to prove that the military profession is an honorable profession. From religious sources, the professional code has elements that justify its missionary zeal, its emphasis on authority and ceremony, and its suffering and hardships.

But it is the sense of fraternity in the military professional code that strikes the sociologist. A sense of intimacy and social solidarity among the officer corps is basic to the professional code. While other professional groups speak of a sense of community, none rivals the military in this respect. Much of military education seems to be concerned with this sense of group solidarity. But clearly after World War II, the military profession experienced a crisis in its sense of professional fraternity. Factors that disrupt fraternity are viewed with great concern by military authorities. Thus the sudden increase in numbers and heterogeneity of social background of Air Force officers has produced a troubled search for an appropriate unifying ethic.[14]

Efforts to improve indoctrination of the professional code have a higher chance of success because the indoctrination process is slow and continuous, and it applies to every aspect of military life. But efforts to explain "why we fight" and to provide a conception of a political goal beyond that of defense of country have been more irrelevant than unsuccessful.

Strategic issues and ideological images are elements of combat effectiveness and organizational control. Although sociologists emphasize the crucial importance of primary group cohesion in military morale, they do not ignore the effects of secondary identifications. Conceptions of the enemy, the strength of nationalism, and the definition of national objectives have varying effects, depending on military realities. For most troops, these symbols are secondary to the immediate social organization of military life, and are filtered through networks of primary group contacts on which individual soldiers depend. Ideological indoctrination may succeed if the image of the enemy and the goals of war can be interpreted in terms that are relevant and meet the day-to-day needs of the individual soldier. When the Nazi propaganda officers spoke of the advantages of national socialism as an ideology, their words fell on deaf ears, but when they mentioned how Hitler had abolished unemployment, they were able to reinforce old loyalties among those who had suffered economic distress.

Moreover, in military organization as in the larger society, there is a small "hard core" of politically oriented persons. These opinion leaders are often more politically alert, concerned with the strategic outline of warfare, and exploit their primary group relationships for indoctrination. In armies of totalitarian states such persons are formally recognized and receive extensive training in political schools and party work. Their equivalents are not regarded as essential for democratic armies, nor can they be expected to develop by a few superficial lectures.[15]

Present evidence offers no basis for assuming that political indoctrination of American troops will make them better fighters or more resistant to Communist indoctrination after capture. By political indoctrination we mean implanting a comprehensive dogma which supplies answers to a wide variety of issues. Such indoctrination of the rank and file of the armed forces in a democratic country may have the opposite effect. As Albert Biderman concludes from his study of Air Force prisoners captured in Korea, resistance to Communist doctrine was lodged in the traditional American negativism toward dogma.[16] Any effort at political indoctrination in order to increase organizational control, or to prepare personnel for resisting Communist indoctrination in the event of capture, may have negative consequences if it undermines the American general distrust of dogmas and makes the men feel inferior because they are uninformed, or feel guilty because they are apolitical, vis-à-vis skilled propagandists.

NOTES TO CHAPTER 5

1. One interesting and highly systematic effort to investigate this problem is James D. Thompson's "Authority and Power in 'Identical' Organizations," *American Journal of Sociology*, vol. 62, November, 1956, pp. 290–301. Dealing with Air Force Squadrons, Thompson demonstrates that differences between the units are due to differences in perceptions of technical operations and not because of personal relations. This study falls into the category of those that fail to take into consideration the special characteristics of military units—the effects of combat goal.

2. Lang, Kurt, "Technology and Career Management in the Military Establishment" in Janowitz, Morris, editor, *The New Military: Changing Patterns of Organization*. Russell Sage Foundation, New York, 1965, pp. 39–81.

3. Lindquist, Ruth, *Marriage and Family Life of Officers and Airmen in a Strategic Air Command Wing*. Technical Report no. 5, Air Force Base Project, Institute for Research in Social Science, University of North Carolina, Chapel Hill, October, 1952.

4. Janowitz, Morris, *The Professional Soldier: A Social and Political Portrait*. The Free Press, Glencoe, Ill., 1960, pp. 40–51.

5. See Chapter 2, Hierarchy and Authority.

6. Lindquist, Ruth, *op. cit.*

7. Janowitz, Morris, *op. cit.*, pp. 175–212.

8. Hunter, Floyd, *Host Community and Air Force Base.* Air Force Base Project, Institute for Research in Social Science, University of North Carolina, Chapel Hill, November, 1952.

9. Biderman, Albert D., "Sequels to a Military Career: The Retired Military Professional" in Janowitz, Morris, editor, *The New Military*, pp. 287–336.

10. Ungerleider, J. T., "The Army, The Soldier, and The Psychiatrist," *American Journal of Psychiatry*, vol. 119, March, 1963, pp. 875–877.

11. Burchard, Waldo W., "Role Conflicts of Military Chaplains," *American Sociological Review*, vol. 19, October, 1954, pp. 528–535.

12. Janowitz, Morris, *op. cit.*, pp. 215–232.

13. *Ibid.*

14. Wolverton, Wallace I., Lt. Col. (Chaplain), *Ethical Judgments of a Group of Air Force Officers*, Air University, Maxwell Air Force Base, Ala., 1950; also *Behavior Standards in USAFE Personnel*, Report no. HR-18, Human Resources Research Institute, Maxwell Air Force Base, Ala., August, 1952.

15. Waldman, Eric, *The Goose Step Is Verboten: The German Army Today.* The Free Press, New York, 1964. This volume contains a discussion of indoctrination in the new Bundeswehr of West Germany.

16. Biderman, Albert D., *Effects of Communist Indoctrination Attempts:* Some Comments Based on an Air Force Prisoners of War Study. Document no. 134247, Air Force Personnel and Training Research Center, Lackland Air Force Base, Texas, September, 1947, p. v.

Chapter 6

THE SOLDIER AND
INTERNATIONAL RELATIONS

By CUSTOM, LAW, AND POLITICAL NECESSITY, the professional soldier must be nonpartisan in domestic political affairs. Yet it is clear that the professional officer requires considerable sensitivity to the political and social consequences of military operations. At each step in the graduated application of force, threatened or actual, to the control of international relations, political and social factors are completely intertwined with what has been called military considerations. In varying degrees this has always been the case. But today military administration permits a very small margin of political and social miscalculation. Assuming an effective form of civilian supremacy, the implementation of military policy is so complex that important political and social tasks tend to adhere to the military even in peacetime.[1] The relations between troops and native civilians in overseas areas, the conduct of counter guerrilla warfare, the management of foreign assistance programs, the implementation of military alliances, and negotiations for arms control, are as much political and social arrangements as they are military operations.

Military leaders in the United States over recent decades have developed a concern for the political and social implications of their behavior. Their concern for these problems does not imply that they have the tradition, knowledge, or the resources at their disposal, to act on the basis of their concerns. Hence, there is little evidence that the American military elite corresponds to the stereotype of a power elite bent on a secret conspiracy. The military elite over the past two decades, like the civilian elite groups, has had to broaden its horizons to include the entire

131

spectrum of international relations. Under these circumstances, the tasks and the responsibilities of the military establishment have been enlarged. It would be in error to describe this process as "designed militarism." Designed militarism—the type identified with Prussian militarism—involves the modification and destruction of civilian institutions by military leaders acting directly and premeditatedly through the state and other institutions.

Equally significant, and more likely to account for crucial aspects of contemporary American problems, is "unanticipated militarism." Unanticipated militarism develops from a lack of effective traditions and practices for controlling the military establishment, as well as from a failure of civilian political leaders to act relevantly and consistently. Under such circumstances a vacuum is created, which not only encourages an extension of the tasks and power of military leadership but actually compels such trends. In the last decade, with the growth in the authority and personnel of the Department of Defense, civilian direction of the military establishment has become more comprehensive, even to the point of raising questions of intrusion into so-called purely military matters.

Nevertheless, the concern of professional officers with the political and social aspects of military operations—in particular with the limitation on force—is likely to continue, for better or for worse. One can say for better, since it could contribute to a rational foreign policy; for worse, because politically sensitive military leadership could be less responsive to civilian control. But any extensive effort by military organization to provide political indoctrination of its members, beyond clarifying strategic concepts and supplying day to day public information, is not appropriate for a political democracy. Such a program is also unlikely to improve military effectiveness.

Political indoctrination in the American military establishment has, of course, been a continuous problem. The essential requirement of maintaining a position of neutrality toward issues with partisan implications is especially difficult in a political democracy. One effect of this requirement has been a restriction of topics discussed to those which have been resolved by consensus and removed from public debate. Such topics are then of such a general and abstract nature that instruction is difficult and produces an apathetic response. But basically, there has been a profound and complete rejection by the military—both officers and enlisted personnel—of political indoctrination.

Congressional concern about political indoctrination in 1962 led to a detailed investigation of the Armed Forces Information and Education programs by a committee appointed by the Secretary of Defense.[2] They concluded that indoctrination had been isolated from other forms of military training, and consequently made an end in itself, of secondary importance to commanders. They recommended that indoctrination be defined as "General Military Training," and that commanders be given the same responsibility for indoctrination as for technical military training. Subjects common to all services were defined as the American political tradition, Communism-in-Action, national policies, and orientations about foreign countries. General Military Training, a responsibility of commanders, would be distinguished from informational services which are provided to a voluntary audience through Armed Forces Radio and Television Service and service periodicals.

NEW PROFESSIONAL PERSPECTIVES

The changed character of international relations presents the professional soldier with the necessity of a new conception of the appropriate means of employing force. The general trend may be described as one of reverse escalation. The prospect of total war dominated the military concept of international relations for a brief period following the explosion of the atomic bomb. With increased recognition of equal enemy capability, a concept of mutual deterrence developed. Limited nuclear warfare was then briefly proposed as an alternative, but the risk was so great that it might develop into unlimited nuclear warfare that it proved to be only a transition back to conventional warfare.

Meanwhile, a decision to employ conventional warfare involved the corresponding risk that it might develop to the point

that nuclear weapons would be employed. This restraint pro-
voked concern with the development of such methods of limited
conventional warfare as irregular warfare, armed subversion, and
resistance by counter-subversion. While such subconventional
methods continue, the persisting threat of nuclear warfare has
produced extensive discussion of the strategy and tactics of
mutual warning, inspection, and disarmament. At this point,
political and social—rather than military—considerations predominate. As a result, changes in doctrine and self-conception of
the military profession are required. Janowitz suggests:

> The use of force in international relations has been so altered that
> it seems appropriate to speak of constabulary forces, rather than of
> military forces. The constabulary concept provides a continuity with
> past military experiences and traditions, but it also offers a basis for
> the radical adaptation of the profession. The military establishment
> becomes a constabulary force when it is continuously prepared to
> act, committed to the minimum use of force, and seeks viable inter-
> national relations, rather than victory, because it has incorporated a
> protective military posture.[3]

The professional soldier is also required to acquire an increasing number of skills and orientations common to civilian administrators and even political leaders. Professionalism as a measure
of adaptation to social change thereby implies that the classic
distinction and tension between the troop commander—the
manager of men and machines and the staff officer—the manager
of plans and coordination—tend to become less clear-cut. If the
preparation for combat requires authority oriented to maintaining initiative among groups and possessing the skills of indirect
control, then the skills of the combat commander and staff officer
are in effect converging. Thus the professional commander becomes more interested in the interpersonal techniques of organization, maintenance of morale, and negotiation.[4]

The effect of these trends is already apparent in the changing
organizational experience of the professional officer. Numerous
senior officers have combined achievement in both spheres of the
military establishment as a result of their experiences in World

War II and the Korean Conflict. Even at lower levels of military organization, activities have grown beyond the traditional categories of platoons, regiments, and staff sections. An entirely new vocabulary of structures has developed, including teams, missions, and projects, as well as boards, committees, and directorates. Officers are likely to spend less time with their own organizations and an increased amount of time in extra-organizational activities. Such activities provide the officer with an area of initiative outside of specific hierarchical control, and involve evaluations by colleagues on the basis of diversified professional situations. He is thus required to develop a new set of skills in the form of committee behavior, resembling those of the political leader: evaluating the relative weight of the recommendations of various staff sections, mustering support and answering counter-arguments, and sensing an incipient consensus.

A similar trend modifying hierarchical organizational conceptions in the Army is apparent in the structure of the "Reorganization Objective Army Division." This formation consists of multiple small specialized and standardized units, designed for flexible and variable alignments within the larger organization. The typical infantry division, for example, contains eight infantry battalions and two tank battalions which can be arranged in various combinations under three autonomous brigade headquarters, with support from specialized cellular units. Hierarchical arrangements are consequently functional and transitory, thus reducing the emphasis on domination and substituting lateral patterns of communication for the traditional vertical pattern.

From the long-range perspective of a career, however, important points of tension persist. Strains are especially prominent in the transition from the emotional and technical requirements of a combat officer assigned to duties at sea, with tactical ground units, or with air crews, to the requirements of higher command. An increasing number of those who survive the rigors of indoctrination, training, and initial assignments, may expect to move on to positions which will require the development of general managerial skills applicable to a wide range of assignments, including politically orientated ones.

An alternative dichotomy of career development is emerging which may separate leaders with broad managerial orientations toward their tasks from those who are primarily concerned with the technical development of new weapons systems. An increasing number of senior officers are now following scientific and technical careers. These scientific specialists tend to have narrow definitions of their tasks and to be relatively unconcerned with the political and social implications of the weapons systems that they promote. With an assured position in the hierarchy and steadily rising prestige in scientific matters, they are frequently permitted to pass judgment on broad professional issues for which their specialized technical experiences have not adequately equipped them. This trend produces new strains in the military establishment and may impede the development of broader perspectives.

Research into career lines and career development in the military establishment is continually required to understand these trends and their consequences. Such research must be broader than personnel selection research and must focus on organizational change. One interesting approach is the analysis of sponsored military literature, as reflecting changes in the professional self-image of the services. In such an analysis, Feld concluded that both Army and Navy have moved from a traditional "primitive self-conception" to a competitive or managerial one. However, there appeared to be a significant divergence between these services: "The Navy has followed a pattern of increased professionalization by stimulating conformity to existing patterns while modifying them slowly. The Army has engaged in a drastic and unstable search for new bases of professional identity."[5]

CONSEQUENCES OF FORCE

Thus far the focus of this study has been on the internal structure of the military establishment as a social system and as a reflection of the larger society. To speak of the consequences of military behavior—the political and social outcomes—requires a broader frame of reference. The military specialist thinks of force as a factor in international relations in absolute quantitative and physical terms—manpower and firepower. The sociologist must assume that military force is but one of several means that a nation state has at its disposal for influencing international relations; others are economic, cultural, and political media, diplomatic negotiation, and mass persuasion. Of crucial importance to the sociologist is the particular organization of these various means, for the same instruments differently organized have different consequences.

For example, military occupation by American forces carrying their own logistical support has had very different political consequences from those resulting from occupation by Russian troops who exploit the local resources. The performance of American military government, from Germany to Korea, was deeply influenced by not only the political directives under which it operated but also by the fact that military government organization was kept strictly parallel to tactical military organization. Consequently, as the front expanded, specific localities were administered by as many as four different units, each having to rebuild its own local contacts. Even after stabilization, or where military government took over major areas directly as in Japan and Korea, the channels of command were unduly complicated by their articulation with occupational units. The arrangement tended to emphasize administrative efficiency at the expense of social and political objectives.

The utilization of a sociological perspective by the military establishment has been limited chiefly to those functions which the military in the past has considered to be secondary functions —political and psychological warfare, military government, and troop indoctrination. With the exception of economics which has emerged as a powerful tool of management, the use of the theoretical and technical capabilities of social scientists in dealing with military problems has been sporadic and infrequent at best, although notable instances can be reported by social scientists. Perhaps the most marked and dramatic shift has been the introduction of sociological materials, especially about the military profession, into the general education of military officers.

The relevance of sociological thinking is not limited to the analysis of consequences of particular military operations. It has a broader relevance for understanding the potentials and limitations on the use of force in all its dimensions as a factor for influencing international relations. Such dimensions include strategic and operational planning, the direction of operations, the consolidation of outcomes, and the assessment of effects. At each point in the cycle, political and sociological assumptions are required and the perspectives of the sociologist are correspondingly relevant.

In the past, the political and sociological assumptions that military planners have made either remained implicit or were limited to their stereotypes as to how soldiers of specific nationalities behaved in battle. These stereotypes often were based on the contacts that professional soldiers developed in the course of their careers as military observers, military attachés, and participants in previous military operations. When nations fought with limited military forces, and the issue at stake was the likely effectiveness of military units in being, such estimates at least supplied some basis for military planning. But as warfare grew to require total involvement of the population, the problem extends well beyond the scope of professional military thinking. The U. S. military services entered World War II unprepared to handle such estimates in their strategical planning. During the course of the hostilities, the evaluation of strategic intelligence was developed to the point that highly sophisticated estimates of the probable behavior of German and Japanese social systems under attack were developed. In retrospect, these estimates had high relevance and validity, although the extent to which they entered into actual strategical planning and operations is most problematical. Many of these estimates were developed by civilian social scientists in uniform and were often the results of self-generated assignments, which ultimately developed some organizational legitimacy.

Since the end of World War II, the necessity for strategic political and social intelligence for guiding national security policy, including military policy, has been generally accepted.

The armed forces even played a role and continue to be active in subsidizing university-based social research on foreign social systems, as for example, the Russian research program of the United States Air Force at Harvard University. By contrast, strategic political military intelligence in the Korean Conflict did not reach the same levels of analysis, because of the difficulties of mobilizing specialized civilian personnel in a period of limited hostilities. While there has been a marked proliferation of country and area type studies concerning the new nations, the systematic analysis of civil-military relations, and the sociology of war and revolution in these areas is only gradually emerging. The theoretical dimensions and practical requirements of strategic intelligence for foreign policy is a topic that evokes strong and passionate opinions among experts, especially in a period of difficult foreign relations, since it is easier to declare that intelligence was faulty than to reevaluate policies.

However, the sociological analysis of total societies is not yet adequately developed to clarify these basic issues. Current sociological analysis tends to view violence in a social system as a form of disorganization or as deviant behavior.[6] It is also important to note that such an orientation is prevalent among social anthropologists, even though a major source of social change among nonliterate social systems has been warfare. As a result, a body of propositions about the conditions under which force maintains and modifies social structure has not yet been developed.

Given the present state of sociological theory, one feasible approach to a more systematic understanding of the role of force in social change is the comparative sociological study of military organization; that is, all types of military organization, including paramilitary forces, guerrilla units, and resistance movements. A model for such research can be found in the analysis of the guerrillas in Malaya by Lucian Pye.[7] An alternative frame of reference is to focus on military elites as a social grouping and to analyze their social composition, career lines, and indoctrination as an index to military behavior.[8] In *The Military in the Political Development of New Nations*, a series of propositions are presented to account for the role of the professional soldier in the politics of some fifty emerging countries. This analysis sees the capacity of the armed forces of these nations to intervene politically as a function of the instruments of violence at their disposal, and the organizational skills of their leaders. Once having seized power, these armed forces have pervasive limitations to serve as a political leadership group.[9]

The patterns of "armed forces and society" in western Europe have been studied to some limited degree on a comparative basis as part of the effort to understand military professionalism and civil-military relations in advanced industrial countries. These studies indicate a broad pattern of uniformity in that the military do not operate as partners of the political leadership, but as pressure groups. At the same time, there are important differences from country to country in the influence of the military as a pressure group and in their professional objectives.[10]

The conduct of military operations requires an economy of effort in order to avoid needless casualties and to maximize the chances of achieving political and social objectives. Force cannot be applied effectively merely in terms of military considerations. With the destructive prospects of atomic warfare, force has meaning only as it relates to efforts at persuasion. The British term "political warfare" is an effort to conceptualize the use of persuasion and propaganda techniques in a military context.

Among Americans there is a belief that the United States has no tradition and skill in international communications in support of its military objectives. The word "propaganda" is thought of as foreign to United States customs and repulsive to United States objectives. Control and effective management of political warfare are most complex for a democratic state. Wide areas of political warfare require an element of secret preparation, at least, and secrecy is disruptive of democratic political control.

However, the United States does have precedents for international political warfare. Imaginative and successful exploitation of persuasive means to achieve military objectives have been used since the Revolutionary War. *A Psychological Warfare Casebook* documents these events and indicates the extent to which social scientific perspectives are relevant for developing principles for conducting psychological warfare.[11] Historically, it was assumed that propaganda could be disseminated only by a few key figures and leaders. Today large staffs, detailed planners, and complex organizations are required for the task. The extensive planning and organization of Soviet communications are described by Schramm and Riley in the Korean and Communist occupation of South Korea.[12]

As long as the military concept of warfare focused on atomic warfare, the official stimulus for research was on the social and psychological aspects of disaster rather than on political and psychological warfare. Most available civilian disasters have been carefully investigated and important observations systematized by Martha Wolfenstein.[13] With the reemergence of limited warfare concepts, questions about the social consequences of military operations are more pertinent. What situations of the past and the present are likely models to clarify future contingencies? The nature of limited warfare since the end of World War II involving Communist forces has obscured the distinction between conventional military operations and police duties. Even the United Nations forces operating in the Israeli-Arab conflict found that more conventional police organization was required to maintain an unstable equilibrium. Communist political doctrine apparently is more compatible with organizational forms equipped to handle the wide variety of missions that limited warfare requires. Thus radical innovations must be developed by professional soldiers when they are required by the political situation.

The analysis of the sociological consequences of limited warfare cannot be understood within the categories now used by the American military establishment. In an effort to accommodate itself to political needs, a number of specialized auxiliaries have been incorporated as staff agencies: psychological warfare personnel, military government specialists, guerrilla warfare teams and special forces. Personnel are also trained for military assistance operations. The effectiveness of these specialists depends on U. S. national policies. The concept that these specialists perform separate technical functions, however, has been a fundamental weakness in their support of military operations. Research on the successes and failures of these politico-military functions in the recent past continues to be essential. This involves an under-standing of how American social structure has influenced the development of our military institutions and how military organ-ization adapts to and resists change. Perhaps one of the most revealing and useful case studies is that of the success and limita-tions of American military government in South Korea by Grant E. Meade, whose analysis penetrates beyond official doctrine into day-to-day operations.[14]

The impact of military operations in South Vietnam has been significant in the extent to which these activities have required a modification of organizational doctrine for dealing with the prob-lems of limited war and guerrilla operations. While there is yet no major social science synthesis of these events or their impact on the armed services, it is clear that the consequences will pervade the United States armed forces in the decades ahead. The dramatic responses to the new requirements range from the creation of Special Forces to deal with guerrilla warfare, to the emergence of the civic action concept in which the military seek to be agents of social change by using their resources for economic and social welfare activities. South Vietnam is thus completing the political education of the professional military officer, a process which was initiated in the Korean Conflict. A series of theoretical essays edited by Harry Eckstein, entitled *Internal Warfare*, seek to supply frameworks for analyzing these processes of social change.[15] But sociological writing on insurrections and counter-insurgency is much too diffuse and relatively uncon-cerned with organizational realities.

The traditional experience of the professional officer has fostered a mechanistic conception of society which recent trends have shown signs of modifying. Military personnel have not had the opportunity to develop local attachments because of the systematic rotation of assignment and residential seclusion in military installations. Consequently, few professional officers have had opportunities to participate in social action which has been generated by local events. The "bargaining" component of the local political process is rarely encountered. Tasks assigned to the military usually imply that the political process has been exhausted, and frequently the professional officer only has an awareness of the political process after there is evidence that it has failed. Hence, he is prone to believe that the political process can be eliminated, or that the same result can be achieved by a more direct method.

The lack of local involvement of the professional officer also cultivates a conception of the political process in its most highly visible aspect: the electoral campaign. As a result, in foreign areas he places an exaggerated reliance on mass communications techniques such as radio and leaflets. The conception of the welfare state as a "vote-getter" rather than a demonstration of the regime's recognition of a social need leads to sporadic distributions of food or demonstrations of modern medical healing in villages which cannot support such services from their own resources. Friendly ambassadors exhort native leaders to move among the people with them, "campaigning" for allegiance to the native regime. Such techniques at times have the effect of sharpening a sense of deprivation and accelerating aspirations beyond the capacity of the native regime to satisfy them.

In the present state of international relations, the military establishment persists in thinking mainly about the implications of future hostilities, insurgent, limited or total. But there is an immediate impact of the worldwide U.S. military system on international relations and worldwide politico-military affairs. The official doctrines of the U.S. military establishment have had important consequences in fashioning Soviet strategy and tactics in the nuclear age.[16] The stationing of troops in allied countries and the creation of new elites and counter-elites by military assistance programs are equally important aspects of military operations. The conduct of military staffs in international alliances speeds up or retards the development of regional political and economic arrangements. The actual deployment of our air forces, and the public statements—threats and reassurances—that military leaders are daily forced to make, constitute for better or worse a most potent ingredient of political warfare.

The United States trains large numbers of foreign military personnel, especially in the borderline areas of the control of guerrilla warfare and para-military operations. More recently, new programs of civic action are being launched, especially in South America, where the American military seek to stimulate their local counterparts to engage in economic development and nation-building. In all of these areas, the military are active agents of social change or can become factors resisting social change.

Some public opinion polling has been conducted on the attitudes of allied populations toward the American troops stationed in their countries. The work of staff members of the Social Science Division of The Rand Corporation has been a notable example of a sustained research contribution to these problems. Research studies from this group include Hans Speier's analysis of the German military elite to remilitarization, and the case study by W. Phillips Davison of the classic use of the military establishment in the cold war, *The Berlin Blockade: A Study in Cold War Politics.*[17]

But sociologists and members of related disciplines have not accepted the responsibility for the systematic study of the impact of the military, as a social system in being, on international relations. Under these circumstances it is understandable that the military has not developed a profound interest in these research matters. Moreover, it would be most undesirable in a democracy if the locus of concern were exclusively or even mainly with the military. If social change, at home and abroad, is a central theme of sociological analysis, the implications are obvious.

NOTES TO CHAPTER 6

1. Janowitz, Morris, editor, *The New Military: Changing Patterns of Organization.* Russell Sage Foundation, New York, 1964, pp. 11–12.

2. *Report to the Secretary of Defense of the Advisory Committee on Nonmilitary Instruction,* Karl R. Bendetsen, Chairman, Washington, July 20, 1962. See also Bowles, Frank H., *The Information Program of the Armed Forces:* A Report of a Project Sponsored by the Fund for the Advancement of Education at the Request of the United States Department of Defense, 1956.

3. Janowitz, Morris, *The Professional Soldier: A Social and Political Portrait.* The Free Press, Glencoe, Ill., 1960, p. 418.

4. Lovell indicates that even in the Academy socialization process there is a shift from heroic to "managerial" orientations, in comparing freshmen with seniors at West Point. See Lovell, John P., "The Professional Socialization of the West Point Cadet," in Janowitz, Morris, editor, *The New Military*, pp. 119–157.

5. Feld, Maury, "The Military Self-Image in a Technological Environment" in Janowitz, Morris, editor, *The New Military*, p. 188.

6. Such a perspective is even to be found by implication in the highly systematic works of Talcott Parsons. See *The Social System*, The Free Press, Glencoe, Ill., 1951.

7. Pye, Lucian W., *Guerrilla Communism in Malaya: Its Social and Political Meaning.* Princeton University Press, Princeton, N.J., 1956.

8. An example of this approach is to be found in Ithiel de Sola Pool's *The Satellite Generals: A Study of Military Elites in the Soviet Sphere.* Stanford University Press, Stanford, Calif., 1955.

9. Janowitz, Morris, *The Military in the Political Development of the New Nations.* University of Chicago Press, Chicago, 1964.

10. See, for example, the series of essays on "The Armed Forces in Western Society," *European Journal of Sociology*, in press, 1965.

11. Daugherty, William E., and Morris Janowitz, *A Psychological Warfare Casebook.* The Johns Hopkins University Press, Baltimore, 1958.

12. Schramm, Wilbur, and John W. Riley, Jr., "Communication in the Sovietized State as Demonstrated in Korea," *American Sociological Review*, vol. 16, December, 1951, pp. 757–766.

13. Wolfenstein, Martha, *Disaster.* The Free Press, Glencoe, Ill., 1957.

14. Meade, Grant E., *American Military Government in Korea.* Columbia University Press, New York, 1951.

15. Eckstein, Harry, editor, *Internal Warfare.* The Free Press, New York, 1964.

16. Garthoff, Raymond, *Soviet Strategy in the Nuclear Age.* Frederick A. Praeger, Inc., New York, 1958.

17. Speier, Hans, *German Rearmament and Atomic War*, Row, Peterson and Co., Evanston, Ill., 1957; Davison, W. Phillips, *The Berlin Blockade: A Study in Cold War Politics*, Princeton University Press, Princeton, N.J., 1958. The Social Science Research Council has established a Committee on National Security Policy, under Professor William Fox, which stimulates and reflects the interest of historians and political scientists in the analysis of the backgrounds of military policy.

REVISED
SELECTED BIBLIOGRAPHY

ABRAHAMSSON, BENGT, *Military Professionalization and Political Power,* Sage Series on Armed Forces and Society, Sage Publications, Beverly Hills, California, 1972.

ANDRZEJEWSKI, STANISLAW, *Military Organization and Society,* Routledge and Kegan Paul, London, 1954.

ARCHIVES EUROPEENES DE SOCIOLOGIE, *Armed Forces and Society in Western Europe,* Vol. 6, 1965, pp. 225-308.

BARNETT, CORELLI, "The Education of Military Elites," *Journal of Contemporary History,* Vol. 2, July 1967.

BE'ENI, ELIEZER, *Army Officers in Arab Politics and Society,* Pall Mall, London, 1970.

BIDERMAN, ALBERT D., *March to Calumny,* Macmillan, New York, 1963.

――― "What Is Military?" in Sol Tax, editor, *The Draft: A Handbook of Facts and Alternatives,* University of Chicago Press, Chicago, 1967, pp. 122-137.

――― "Where Do They Go from Here—Retired Military in America," *Annals of the American Academy of Political and Social Science,* 406, March 1973, pp. 146-161.

BIDWELL, CHARLES, "The Young Professional in the Army," *American Sociological Review,* Vol. 26, June 1961, pp. 360-372.

BIENEN, HENRY, editor, *The Military Intervenes: Case Studies in Political Development,* Russell Sage Foundation, New York, 1968.

BIGLER, R. R., *Der einsame Soldat: eine soziologische Deutung der militarischen Organisation,* Frauenfeld: Verlag Huber, 1963.

BLAKE, JOSEPH A., "The Organization as Instrument of Violence: The Military Case," *Sociological Quarterly,* Vol. 11, Summer 1970, pp. 331-350.

BOGART, LEO, *Social Research and the Desegregation of the U.S. Army,* Markham, Chicago, 1969.

BOWERS, R. V., "The Military Establishment," in P. F. Lazarsfeld, W. H. Sewell, and H. L. Wilensky, editors, *The Uses of Sociology,* Basic Books, New York, 1967, pp. 234-274.

BRAGULAT, JULIO BUSQUETS, *El Militar de Carrera en Espana: Estudio de Sociologia Militar,* Ediciones Ariel, Barcelona, 1967.

BROWN, C. S., "The Social Attitudes of American Generals, 1898-1940," unpublished doctoral dissertation, University of Wisconsin, Madison, 1951.

BURCHARD, WALDO W., "Role Conflicts of Military Chaplains," *American Sociological Review,* Vol. 19, October 1954, pp. 528-535.

CHESLER, DAVID J., NIEL J. VAN STEENBERG, and JOYCE E. BRUECKEL, "Effect on Morale of Infantry Team Replacement and Individual Replacement Systems," *Sociometry,* Vol. 18, December 1955, pp. 587-597.

CHRISTIE, RICHARD, "An Experimental Study of Modification in Factors Influencing Recruits' Adjustment to the Army," Research Center for Human Relations, New York University, 1953 (mimeographed).

CLARK, RODNEY A., "Leadership in Rifle Squads on the Korean Front Line," Technical Report No. 21, Human Research Unit No. 2, Fort Ord, California, undated.

COATES, C. H., and R. J. PELLEGRIN, *Military Sociology: A Study of American Institutions and Military Life,* Social Science Press, University Park, Maryland, 1965.

COHEN, STEPHEN P., *The Indian Army: Its Contribution to the Development of a Nation,* University of California Press, Berkeley, 1971.

COLES, H. L., editor, *Total War and Cold War: Problems in Civilian Control of the Military,* Ohio State University Press, Columbus, 1962.

CUTRIGHT, PHILLIPS, *A Pilot Study of Factors in Economic Success or Failure: Based on Selective Service and Social Security Records,* U.S. Department of Health, Education, and Welfare, Social Security Administration, Washington, June 1964.

DAUGHERTY, WILLIAM E., and MORRIS JANOWITZ, *A Psychological Warfare Casebook,* Johns Hopkins University Press, Baltimore, 1958.

DAVIS, ARTHUR K., "Bureaucratic Patterns in the Navy Officer Corps," *Social Forces,* Vol. 27, December 1948, pp. 143-153.

DAVIS, J. W., Jr., and K. M. DOLBEARE, *Little Groups of Neighbors: The Selective Service System,* Markham, Chicago, Illinois, 1968.

DAVISON, W. PHILLIPS, *The Berlin Blockade: A Study in Cold War Politics,* Princeton University Press, Princeton, New Jersey, 1958.

DEMETER, KARL, *Das Deutsche Heer und Seine Offiziere,* Verlag von Reimar, Hobbing, Berlin, 1935.

DICKS, HENRY V., "The International Soldiers—A Psychiatrist's View," in Lincoln P. Bloomfield, with Edward H. Bowan et al., *International Military Forces: The Question of Peacekeeping in an Armed and Disarming World,* Little, Brown, Canada, 1964.

DICKS, H. V., E. A. SHILS, and H. S. DINERSTEIN, *Service Conditions and Morale in the Soviet Armed Forces: A Pilot Study,* Volume 1 of *The Soviet Army,* U.S. Air Force Project, Rand Corporation R-213, Santa Monica, California, August 25, 1951.

DUBUISSON, A. U., and W. A. KLIEGER, "Combat Performance of Enlisted Men with Disciplinary Records," Technical Research Note 148, U.S. Army Personnel Research Office, Washington, 1964.

EVAN, W., "Due Process of Law in Military and Industrial Organization," *Administrative Science Quarterly,* Vol. 7, 1962, pp. 187-207.

FELD, MAURY, "A Typology of Military Organization," *Public Policy,* Vol. 7, 1958.

FINER, S. E., *The Man on Horseback: The Role of the Military in Politics,* Praeger, New York, 1962.

FRANKLIN, JOHN HOPE, *The Militant South, 1800-1861,* Belknap Press of Harvard University Press, Cambridge, Massachusetts, 1956.

GENSCHEL, DIETRICH, *Wehrreform und Reaktion: Die Vorbeitung der Innere Führung, 1951-1956,* R. V. Decker's Verlag G. Schenck, Hamburg, 1972.

GINZBERG, ELI et al., *The Ineffective Soldier: The Lost Divisions,* Columbia University Press, New York, 1959.

GIRARDET, R., editor, *La Crise Militaire Francaise 1945-1962: Aspects Sociologiques et Ideologiques,* A. Colin, Paris, 1964.

GITTING, JOHN, *The Role of the Chinese Army,* Oxford University Press, London, 1967.

GOLDMAN, NANCY, "The Changing Role of Women in the Armed Forces," *American Journal of Sociology,* Vol. 78, January 1973, pp. 892-911.

GRINKER, ROY E., and JOHN SPIEGEL, *Men Under Stress,* Blakiston, Philadelphia, 1945.

HAUSMAN, WILLIAM, and DAVID M. RIOCH, "Military Psychiatry," *Archives of General Psychiatry,* Vol. 16, 1967, pp. 727-739.

HENRY, ANDREW F., and EDGAR F. BORGATTA, "A Comparison of Attitudes of Enlisted and Commissioned Air Force Personnel," *American Sociological Review,* Vol. 18, December 1953, pp. 669-671.

HENRY, ANDREW F., JOHN W. MASLAND, and LAURENCE I. RADWAY, "Armed Forces Unification and the Pentagon Officer," *Public Administration Review,* Vol. 15, Summer 1955, pp. 173-180.

HILSMAN, R., *Strategic Intelligence and National Decisions,* Free Press, New York, 1956.

HOMANS, GEORGE C., "The Small Warship," *American Sociological Review,* Vol. 11, June 1946, pp. 294-300.

HOROWITZ, I. L., "The Military Elites" in S. M. Lipset, and Aldo Solari, editors, *Elites in Latin America,* Oxford University Press, New York, 1967, pp. 146-189.

"HUMAN BEHAVIOR IN MILITARY SOCIETY," special issue of the *American Journal of Sociology,* Vol. 51, March 1946, pp. 359-508.

HUNTER, FLOYD, "Host Community and Air Force Base," Air Force Base Project, Institute for Research in Social Science, University of North Carolina, Chapel Hill, November 1952.

HUNTINGTON, SAMUEL P., *The Soldier and the State,* Harvard University Press, Cambridge, Massachusetts, 1957.

――― editor, *Changing Patterns of Military Politics,* Free Press, New York, 1962.

――― *Political Order in Changing Societies,* Yale University Press, New Haven, Connecticut, 1968.

JANOWITZ, MORRIS, "Military Elites and the Study of War," *Journal of Conflict Resolution,* Vol. 1, March 1957, pp. 9-18.

――― "Changing Patterns of Organizational Authority: The Military Establishment," *Administrative Science Quarterly,* Vol. 3, March 1959, pp. 473-493.

――― *The Professional Soldier: A Social and Political Portrait,* Free Press, Glencoe, Illinois, 1960, 1971.

――― *The Military in the Political Development of New Nations: An Essay in Comparative Analysis,* University of Chicago Press, Chicago, 1964.

――― editor, *The New Military: Changing Patterns of Organization,* Russell Sage Foundation, New York, 1964. Includes the following papers: Kurt Lang, "Technology and Career Management in the Military Establishment;" Oscar Grusky, "The Effects of Succession: A Comparative Study of Military and Business Organization;" John P. Lovell, "The Professional Socialization of the West Point Cadet;" Maury D. Feld, "Military Self-Image in a Technological Environment;" Roger W. Little, "Buddy Relations and Combat Performance;" Richard W. Seaton, "Deterioration of Military Work Groups Under Deprivation Stress;" Mayer N. Zald and William Simon, "Career Opportunities and Commitments Among Officers;" Albert D. Biderman, "Sequels to a Military Career: The Retired Military Professional;" Moshe Lissak, "Selected Literature on Revolutions and Coups d'Etat in the Developing Nations."

――― "Volunteer Armed Forces and Military Purpose," *Foreign Affairs,* April 1972, pp. 422-443.

――― "The U.S. Forces and the Zero Draft," *Adelphi Papers,* No. 94, 1973.

JANOWITZ, MORRIS, and JACQUES VAN DOORN, editors, *On Military Intervention,* Rotterdam University Press, Rotterdam, 1971.

——— editors, *On Military Ideology,* Rotterdam University Press, Rotterdam, 1971.

JOFFE, E., "Party and Army: Professionalism and Political Control in the Chinese Officer Corps, 1949-1964," East Asian Monographs, No. 19, Harvard University, Cambridge, Massachusetts, 1965.

JOHNSON, JOHN J., editor, *The Role of the Military in Underdeveloped Countries,* Princeton University Press, Princeton, New Jersey, 1962.

JOHNSTON, JEROME, and JERALD G. BACKMAN, "Young Men and Military Service," Vol. V of *Youth in Transition,* Institute for Social Research, University of Michigan, Ann Arbor, 1972.

KARSTEN, PETER, *The Naval Aristrocracy,* Free Press, New York, 1972.

KELLEHER, CATHERINE, editor, *Political Military Systems: A Comparative Perspective,* Sage Research Progress Series on War, Revolution, and Peacekeeping, Vol. IV, Sage Publications, Beverly Hills, California, 1974.

KLASSEN, ALBERT D., Jr., "Military Service in American Life since World War II: An Overview," Report No. 117, National Opinion Research Center, University of Chicago, Chicago, September 1966.

KLIEGER, W. A., A. U. DUBUISSON, and B. B. SARGENT, "Correlates of Disciplinary Record in a Wide-Range Sample," Technical Research Note 125, U.S. Army Personnel Research Office, Washington, 1962.

KOLKOWICZ, ROMAN, *The Soviet Military and the Communist Party,* Princeton University Press, Princeton, New Jersey, 1967.

KORPI, W., *Social Pressures and Attitudes in Military Training,* Almqvist and Wiksell, Stockholm, 1964.

KOSSOK, M., "Armee und Politik in Lateinamerika" (Army and Politics in Latin America), in *Die nationale Freiheitsbewegung 1965, Bilanz, Berichte, Chronik,* Karl-Marx Universität, Leipzig, 1966, pp. 135-161.

KRIESBERG, L., editor, *Social Process in International Relations.* John Wiley, New York, 1968.

LAMMERS, C. J., "Een sociologische analyse van de inlijving van groepen adspirant officieren in de seemacht" in *Het Koninklkjk Institut Voor de Marine,* University of Amsterdam, Amsterdam, 1963.

LANG, KURT, "Military Career Structure: Emerging Trends and Alternatives," *Administrative Science Quarterly,* Vol. 17, December 1972, pp. 487-497.

——— *Military Institutions and the Sociology of War; a Review of the Literature with Annotated Bibliography,* Sage Series on Armed Forces and Society, Sage Publications, Beverly Hills, California, 1972.

——— "Military Sociology: a Trend Report and Bibliography," *Current Sociology 13,* 1, 1965, pp. 155.

LASSWELL, H. D., "The Garrison State," *American Journal of Sociology,* Vol. 46, 1941, pp. 455-468.

LEIGHTON, ALEXANDER H., *Human Relations in a Changing World,* E. P. Dutton, New York, 1949.

LEWIS, MICHAEL A., *England's Sea-Officers: The Story of the Naval Profession,* Allen and Unwin, London, 1939.

LIEBERSON, STANLEY, "An Empirical Study of Military-Industrial Linkages," in *American Journal of Sociology,* Vol. 76, No. 4, January 1971.

LIEUWEN, E., *Arms and Politics in Latin America* (rev. ed.), Praeger, New York, 1961.

LIFTON, ROBERT JAY, *Home from the War: Vietnam Veterans: Neither Victims nor Executioners,* Simon and Schuster, New York, 1973.

LINDQUIST, RUTH, "Marriage and Family Life of Officers and Airmen in a Strategic Air Command Wing," Technical Report No. 5, Air Force Base Project, Institute for Research in Social Science, University of North Carolina, Chapel Hill, October 1952.

LITTLE, ROGER WILLIAM, "A Study of the Relationship Between Collective Solidarity and Combat Role Performance," unpublished doctoral dissertation, Michigan State University, East Lansing, 1955.

——— editor, *Handbook of Military Institutions,* Sage Series on Armed Forces and Society, Sage Publications, Beverly Hills, California, 1971. Includes the following chapters: Morris Janowitz, "Military Organization;" Harold Wool, "Military Manpower Procurements and Supply;" Paul D. Nelson, "Personnel Performance Prediction;" Albert D. Biderman, "The Retired Military;" Morris Janowitz, "Basic Education and Youth Socialization in the Armed Forces;" Amos A. Jordan, Jr., "Officer Education;" Roger W. Little, "The Military Family;" Charles Moskos, Jr., "Minority Groups in Military Organization;" Alexander L. George, "Primary Groups, Organization, and Military Performance;" Bernard J. Wiest and Donald A. Devis, "Psychiatric and Social Work Services;" Amos A. Jordan, Jr., "Troop Information and Indoctrination;" William Kornhauser, "Revolutions;" Franklin Mark Osanka, "Social Dynamics of Revolutionary Guerrilla Warfare;" Konrad Kellen, "Psychological Warfare;" Paul W. Blackstock, "Covert Military Operations;" Martin Blumerson, "On the Function of the Military in Civil Disorders;" General Bibliography; and Selected Manpower Statistics.

—— editor, *Selective Service in American Society,* Russell Sage Foundation, New York, 1969.

LOWRY, RICHARD P., "To Arms: Changing Military Roles and the Military Industrial Complex," *Social Problems,* Vol. 18, 1970, pp. 3-16.

LUCKHAM, ROBIN, *The Nigerian Military: A Sociological Analysis of Authority and Revolt, 1960-67,* Cambridge University Press, Cambridge, 1971.

LYONS, GENE M., and JOHN W. MASLAND, *Education and Military Leadership: A Study of the ROTC,* Princeton University Press, Princeton, New Jersey, 1959.

MACK, RAYMOND W., "Social Stratification on U.S. Air Force Bases," Technical Report No. 4, Air Force Base Project, Institute for Research in Social Science, University of North Carolina, Chapel Hill, undated.

MANDELBAUM, DAVID G., *Soldier Groups and Negro Soldiers,* University of California Press, Berkeley, California, 1952.

—— "Psychiatry in Military Society," *Human Organization,* Vol. 13, Fall 1954, pp. 5-15; Winter 1955, pp. 19-25.

MARLOWE, DAVID H., "The Basic Training Process" in Kenneth L. Artiss, editor, *The Symptom as Communication in Schizophrenia,* Grune and Stratton, New York, 1959, pp. 75-98.

MARSHALL, S.L.A., *Men Against Fire,* William Morrow, New York, 1947.

MARWALD, A., "The German General Staff: Model of Military Organization," *Orbis,* Vol. 3, 1959, p. 56.

MASLAND, JOHN W., and LAURENCE I. RADWAY, *Soldiers and Scholars,* Princeton University Press, Princeton, New Jersey, 1957.

MATTICK, HANS W., "Parole to the Army: A Research Report on Felons Paroled to the Army During World War II," presented at the Eighty-seventh Annual Congress of Corrections, Chicago, August 1957.

MAYER, A. J., and T. F. HOULT, "Social Stratification and Combat Survival," *Social Forces,* Vol. 34, December 1955, pp. 155-159.

MEADE, GRANT E., *American Military Government in Korea,* Columbia University Press, New York, 1951.

MERTON, ROBERT K., and PAUL F. LAZARSFELD, editors, *Studies in the Scope and Method of "The American Soldier,"* Free Press, Glencoe, Illinois, 1950.

MILLIS, WALTER and JAMES REAL, *The Abolition of War,* Macmillan, New York, 1963.

MILLS, C. W., *The Power Elite,* Oxford University Press, New York, 1956.

MOSKOS, CHARLES C., Jr., *The American Enlisted Man,* Russell Sage Foundation, New York, 1970.

—— editor, *Public Opinion and the Military Establishment,* Sage Research Progress Series on War, Revolution, and Peacekeeping, Vol. I, Sage Publications, Beverly Hills, California, 1971.

—— "Racial Integration in the Armed Forces," *American Journal of Sociology,* Vol. 72, 1966, pp. 132-148.

—— "The Emergent Military: Civil, Traditional or Plural?" *Pacific Sociological Review,* Vol. 16, April 1973, pp. 255-280.

MYER, SAMUEL, and ALBERT D. BIDERMAN, *Mass Behavior in Battle and Captivity,* University of Chicago Press, Chicago, 1968.

NORMAN, E. H., *Soldier and Peasant in Japan: The Origins of Conscription,* Institute of Pacific Relations, New York, 1943.

NOTTINGHAM, E. K., "Towards an Analysis of the Effects of Two World Wars on the Role and Status of Middle Class Women in the English Speaking World," *American Sociological Review,* Vol. 12, 1947, pp. 666-675.

PAGE, CHARLES H., "Bureaucracy's Other Face," *Social Forces,* Vol. 25, October 1946, pp. 88-94.

PIKE, DOUGLAS EUGENE, *Viet Cong: the Organization and Techniques of the National Liberation Front of South Vietnam,* MIT Press, Cambridge, Massachusetts, 1966.

PILISUK, M., and T. HAYDEN, "Is There a Military Industrial Complex Which Prevents Peace?" *Journal of Social Issues,* Vol. 21, 1965, pp. 67-117.

PIPPING, K., "The Social Life of a Machine Gun Company," *Acta Academiae Aboensis Humaniora,* Vol. 17, 1947.

POOL, ITHIEL DE SOLA et al., *The Satellite Generals: A Study of Military Elites in the Soviet Sphere,* Stanford University Press, Stanford, California, 1955.

PYE, LUCIAN W., *Guerrilla Communism in Malaya: Its Social and Political Meaning,* Princeton University Press, Princeton, New Jersey, 1956.

"REPORT OF THE WORKING GROUP ON HUMAN BEHAVIOR UNDER CONDITIONS OF MILITARY SERVICE: A Joint Project of the Research and Development Board and the Personnel Policy Board in the Office of the Secretary of Defense," Washington, June 1951.

RYAN, F. J., *Relation of Performance to Social Background Factors of Army Inductees,* Catholic University Press, Washington, 1958.

SARKESIAN, SAM C., editor, *The Military-Industrial Complex: A Reassessment,* Sage Research Progress Series on War, Revolution, and Peacekeeping, Vol. II, Sage Publications, Beverly Hills, 1972.

SCHEIN, E. H., "The Chinese Indoctrination Program for Prisoners of War: A Study of Attempted 'Brainwashing'," *Psychiatry,* Vol. 19, 1956, pp. 149-172.

SCHELLING, THOMAS C., "A Special Surveillance Force," in I. Wright, W. M. Evan, and D. Morton, editors, *Preventing World War III,* Simon and Schuster, New York, 1962.

——— *Arms and Influence,* Yale University Press, New Haven, Connecticut, 1966.

SCHMITTER, PHILIPPE, *Military Rule in Latin America: Function, Consequences and Perspectives,* Sage Research Progress Series on War, Revolution, and Peacekeeping, Vol. III, Sage Publication, Beverly Hills, 1973.

SEGAL, D. R., "Selective Promotion in Officer Cohorts," *Sociological Quarterly,* Vol. 8, 1967, pp. 199-206.

SELVIN, HANAN CHARLES, *The Effects of Leadership,* Free Press, Glencoe, Illinois, 1960.

SHARP, LAURE, and ALBERT D. BIDERMAN, *The Employment of Retired Military Personnel,* Bureau of Social Science Research, Inc., Washington, D.C., 1966.

SHARTLE, C. L., "Studies in Naval Leadership: Part I" in Harold S. Guetzkow, editor, *Groups, Leadership and Men,* Carnegie Press, Pittsburgh, 1951, pp. 119-133; reissued in 1963 by Russell and Russell, New York.

SHILS, EDWARD S., and MORRIS JANOWITZ, "Cohesion and Disintegration in the Wehrmacht in World War II," *Public Opinion Quarterly,* Vol. 12, Summer 1948, pp. 280-315.

SODEUR, W., *Wirkungen des Führungsverhaltens in kleinen Formalgruppen,* Meisenhein and Glan, Anto Hain, 1972.

SPEIER, HANS, *Social Order and the Risks of War,* George W. Stewart, New York, 1952.

――― *German Rearmament and Atomic War,* Row, Peterson, Evanston, Illinois, 1957.

STANTON, M. DUNCAN, "The Soldier," in D. Speigel and P. Keith-Spiegel, editors, *Outsiders USA,* Rinehart, San Francisco, 1973, pp. 470-502.

STEPAN, ALFRED, *The Military in Politics: Changing Patterns in Brazil,* Princeton University Press, Princeton, New Jersey, 1971.

STOUFFER, SAMUEL A. et al., *The American Soldier,* Vols. 1 and 2, Princeton University Press, Princeton, New Jersey, 1949.

SUCHMAN, EDWARD A., ROBIN M. WILLIAMS, Jr., and ROSE K. GOLDSEN, "Student Reaction to Impending Military Service," *American Sociological Review,* Vol. 18, June 1953, pp. 293-304.

TAX, SOL, editor, *The Draft: a Handbook of Facts and Alternatives,* University of Chicago Press, Chicago and London, 1967.

THOMPSON, JAMES D., "Authority and Power in 'Identical' Organizations," *American Journal of Sociology,* Vol. 62, November 1956, pp. 290-301.

TURNER, RALPH H., "The Naval Disbursing Officer as a Bureaucrat," *American Sociological Review,* Vol. 12, June 1947, pp. 342-348.

UNGERLEIDER, J. T., "The Army, The Soldier, and The Psychiatrist," *American Journal of Psychiatry,* Vol. 119, March 1963, pp. 875-877.

U.S. CONGRESS, SENATE COMMITTEE ON ARMED SERVICES, *A Study of the Military Retired Pay System and Certain Related Subjects,* Eighty-seventh Congress, First Session, Government Printing Office, Washington, 1961.

UYEKI, EUGENE S., "Draftee Behavior in the Cold-War Army," *Social Problems,* Vol. 8, Fall 1960, pp. 151-158.

VAGTS, ALFRED, *A History of Militarism,* W. W. Norton, New York, 1937.

VAN DOORN, JACQUES, editor, *Armed Forces and Society,* Mouton, The Hague, 1968.

——— editor, *Military Professions and Military Regimes,* Mouton, The Hague, 1969.

VAN RIPER, P. P., and D. B. UNWALLA, "Voting Patterns Among High-Ranking Military Officers," *Political Science Quarterly,* Vol. 80, 1965, pp. 48-61.

VATIKOTIS, P. J., *"The Egyptian Army in Politics: Pattern for New Nations?"* Indiana University Press, Bloomington, 1961.

WAMSLEY, GARY, "Contrasting Institutions of Air Force Socialization: Happenstance or Bellwether?" *American Journal of Sociology,* Vol. 78, September 1972, pp. 399-417.

WHITSON, WILLIAM, *The Chinese High Command,* Praeger, New York, 1973.

WIATR, J. J., *Armia i spoleczenstwo: wprowadzenie do socjologi wojska,* Wydawnictwo Ministerstwa Obrony Narodowej, Warsaw, 1960.

——— *Socjologia wojska* (Military Sociology), Wydawnictwo Ministerstwa Obrony Narodoweij, Warsaw, 1964.

WILENSKY, HAROLD L., *Organizational Intelligence,* Basic Books, New York, 1967.

WILLIAMS, RICHARD HAYS, "Human Factors in Military Operations: Some Applications of the Social Sciences to Operations Research." Technical Memorandum ORO-T-259, Operations Research Office, Chevy Chase, Maryland, 1954 (mimeographed).

WOLFE, J. N., and JOHN ERICKSON, editors, *The Armed Services and Society: Alienation, Management, and Integration,* University Press, Edinburgh, undated.

WOLVERTON, WALLACE I., "Ethical Judgments of a Group of Air Force Officers," Air University, Maxwell Air Force Base, Alabama, 1950.

WOOL, HAROLD, *The Military Specialist,* Johns Hopkins Press, Baltimore, Maryland, 1968.

YARMONLINSKY, ADAM, *The Military Establishment: Its Impacts on American Society,* Harper and Row, New York, 1971.